San-ch'ü

San-ch'ü
Its Technique and Imagery

WAYNE SCHLEPP

THE UNIVERSITY OF WISCONSIN PRESS

Madison, Milwaukee, and London 1970

55428

Published by

THE UNIVERSITY OF WISCONSIN PRESS

Box 1379, Madison, Wisconsin 53701

The University of Wisconsin Press, Ltd.

27—29 Whitfield Street, London, W.1

Copyright © 1970

by the Regents of the University of Wisconsin

Printed in the United States of America by
Cushing-Malloy, Inc., Ann Arbor, Michigan

SBN 299-05540-X; LC 76-106037

With fondest love
to
Katie and Vaughan

Contents

Preface

It was during my years in the School of Oriental and African Studies, just after I became aware that knowing words and syntax was not sufficient to the task of translating Chinese poetry, that I became interested in the ways in which the Chinese language creates poetic effects. It was suggested by the late Dr. Waley that Yüan dynasty popular verse would serve as good material for a study of poetic effects in Chinese, so I began reading *san-ch'ü*. At that time I had the good fortune to be studying under Ch'eng Hsi, an expert on Yüan drama, with whom I read dozens of *san-ch'ü* as well as a great amount of other poetry. The work on this book was begun under the supervision of Dr. K. P. K. Whitaker. Because of her patience with my endless questions and her ability to convey to me her own appreciation of Chinese poetry, she has my most particular gratitude.

After I returned to America, a grant in 1965 from the Graduate School of the University of Wisconsin allowed me further work on figures of speech. Later, in 1967, through a joint grant from the Graduate School and the American Council of Learned Societies, I was able to read about music theory in hopes of better understanding the nature of Chinese verse composed to music. In 1968 Chapter 1 appeared in *Wenlin: Studies in the Chinese Humanities*, edited by Professor T. T. Chow. For permission to reprint that material here in slightly revised form, I would like to make acknowledgment to the University of Wisconsin Press.

I wish I could thank individually all who have given me their time and help. In particular I want to thank Professor Chow for his most helpful advice and for the calligraphy in the title and Mrs. Kang Chao for writing all the characters in the text. Special thanks are due Hugh Stimson of Yale for his valuable suggestions and the many corrections he made to the transcriptions.

Lake Kegonsa, Wisconsin   W. S.
November, 1969

San-ch'ü

Introduction

San-ch'ü is in the tradition of verse written to song music, a tradition that extends the full breadth of Chinese literature, and is the name given to a corpus of such verse written during the Yüan dynasty when China was under Mongol rule (1234—1368).[1] The music of san-ch'ü was the popular song heard in marketplaces, brothels, or wherever people gathered. In this the Yüan differs little from any other age, and san-ch'ü, like the song verse of Sung, T'ang, and earlier times, was a living form whose language was close to the language of the streets. It stood in the practice of versifying alongside the more careful art of the scholars whose tastes ran to the older forms perfected in T'ang and Sung with a language no longer current as a spoken means of communication.

As popular verse, san-ch'ü attracted the talents of many gifted versifiers. The themes were the result either of enjoyable pastime or, in the hands of some, of imagination and deep thought. The form lent

---

1. The term *ch'ü* (or *ch'ü-tzu* 曲子) originally referred to the song music; another term, *tz'u* 詞, was used to designate the words that were set to the music. The main corpus of song verse that has come down from the T'ang and Sung dynasties is called tz'u and what we now call san-ch'ü were still called tz'u during the Yüan. It was only later that ch'ü came to refer not to song music but to the song verse that was preserved from Yüan times, most probably through expanded usage in the treatises of Ming and Ch'ing times in which the term came to cover loosely both verse and music. Later, as the music of Yüan went out of currency, all that was left of Yüan song verse were several collections of verse, and the term ch'ü, or san-ch'ü, was used to set this verse off from the song verse of the T'ang and Sung periods.

3

itself to nearly any treatment; as in the centuries before, there were
gay songs, love songs, songs of personal tribulation or public suffering, of satire, of ridicule, songs of nostalgia inevitably touched
with ubi sunt, and a great many on the theme of escape from the pres-
sures of the times, a theme close to our own day. As san-ch'ü attracted more and more writers, its style of language, as well as its
themes, broadened, and while the colloquial or near colloquial remained a style current among Yüan writers, there gradually appeared,
as one would expect, more san-ch'ü in a style whose literary flavor
suggested verse written by the educated practitioners of the old T'ang
and Sung forms of verse.

The Genre

The place of Yüan san-ch'ü in the tradition of song verse is ob-
scured by certain problems that have yet to be fully considered by
literary historians. One such problem is extrinsic to verse and concerns the nature of verse collection and transmission. It seems a
waste of effort to press the truism that verse collection and transmission in China was sporadic. Nonetheless, historians keep labor-
ing under the delusion that the pieces of writing which have come
down to us represent perfectly what was written in the past, with the
result that the possibility of hidden trends and developments is rarely
considered.

Another such problem concerns phenomena within the verse itself
which can indicate development through time. The isolation of such
phenomena is rather difficult because it would require a systematic
method for dealing with form and style, and unfortunately a rigorous
stylistic has not yet been born.

The passages on literary development in histories of Chinese literature rarely emphasize individuality of types of verse. Notions of
origins stem from the view that Chinese poetry is a succession of
separate types, each having risen like the phoenix out of the ashes
of the previous type. The following brief chronology of Chinese poetry by Wang Shih-chen (1526–1570) is typical and represents the
views of writers in Ming and Ch'ing times:

> After the decline of the Three-hundred Odes, there came the *sao*
> 騷 style and *fu* 賦; when it became difficult for sao and fu to be
> set to music, the old *yüeh-fu* 樂府 appeared; after the yüeh-fu
> were no longer popular, the T'ang *chüeh-chü* 絕句 took their place;
> after chüeh-chü had gone its course for a short time, *tz'u* 詞 ap-
> peared; when tz'u no longer pleased the ears of the northerners,
> *pei ch'ü* 北曲 [i.e., Yüan ch'ü] came forth, and as pei ch'ü did not
> accord with the tastes of the southerners, there was *nan ch'ü* 南曲.[2]

2. Wang Shih-chen, *Ch'ü tsao*, p. 27 (full citations will be found
in the Bibliography). A similar chronology by Wang Chi-te (d. 1623),

This view of history does not take into account that the type names designate bodies of verse preserved, not necessarily because of their uniqueness as a type of poetry, but as often because of political and economic circumstances. That is to say, there may or may not have been the leisure and wherewithal to print works in quantities sufficient to assure their preservation. The sporadic nature of verse transmission is thus taken to represent the manner in which verse has developed. This is the problem that Liu Ta-chieh tries to resolve in his discussion of the birth of ch'ü:

> Tz'u [i.e., tz'u of the T'ang period] rose from the people and was taken up by the singing girls and performers. As the verses were convenient for the expression of the emotions and were singable, they became in fact a kind of common literature. During the Five Dynasties (907—960) and the Northern (960—1127) and Southern Sung (1127—1279), scholarly writers [of tz'u] increased and the form became stricter, upon which writers grew meticulous with tones [i.e., meter] and rhetoric until the tz'u . . . became the sole property of the literati. . . . not only were the people unable to read or sing it; even those who were not specialists in the study of tz'u could hardly touch it. . . . While tz'u was becoming more and more rigid and formalized, the singing girls and performers in cities and towns were by no means silenced. They had to sing for a living as before, unburdening their feelings in song, and so in the old songs they sought change, and from the new tunes that had risen from the people they sought themes and material. Out of this labor of renewing was the ch'ü-tzu gradually born. Then the music masters corrected the music[3] and the literati improved poetic diction. Afterwards there were more ch'ü writers. Ch'ü flourished and gradually developed into a form that was different from tz'u and became the new literature that rose in succession to tz'u.[4]

Ch'ü lü, i, pp. 55—56, not quoted here because of its length, is interesting because it does not mention the odes or the Ch'u-tz'u but confines its many illustrative examples to song verse that is still, at least supposedly, closely linked to melody.

3. 正譜 *cheng-p'u*—to compile correct examples of tunes and notate them either according to a system of musical notation or merely by citing a text which seems best to fit the tune.

4. Liu Ta-chieh, *Chung-kuo wen-hsüeh fa-chan shih*, 3:4—5. Other expressions of the view that san-ch'ü owes its rise to the decline of Sung tz'u are: Luo Chin-t'ang, CKSCS, p. 6; Fu Li-p'u, *Chung-kuo yün-wen kai lun*, p. 232; *Chung-kuo wen-hsüeh shih*, p. 787; Cheng Chen-to, *Chung-kuo su wen-hsüeh shih*, pp. 155—56 (however in his illustrated *Chung-kuo wen-hsüeh shih*, pp. 727—29, the discussion of history is better balanced and is most profitable reading, brief as it is). Cheng Ch'ien, *Ts'ung shih tao ch'ü*, pp. 58—65, for

He works under the assumption that each corpus of verse is descended in a direct line from the previous one. Such an assumption, considering the general neglect of folk material, to say nothing of the effect of political and economic change upon verse collection and transmission in general, is very much like assuming one can map a vast country merely by traveling its length on the only road left out of the many that once existed. If there had been, which unfortunately there has not, a consistent transmission of verse, colloquial and literary, and if it had been from a balanced sampling of cultural centers, the extant verse would not give the fragmentary picture we now have, and the development of verse might possibly be as regular as Liu Ta-chieh assumes it to be. There would be none of the rifts that now appear because of political and economic upheaval nor would there then be any need to explain the origins of a corpus of verse that happened to be preserved in one period in terms of a corpus of verse preserved in the previous period.

The rift that appears between tz'u and ch'ü is most easily explained in terms other than direct literary development. Commerce between the Southern Sung and the Liao (904–1125) and Chin (1115–1234) kingdoms did not flow freely for a century and a half and so the song verse that was popular in China after the time of partition developed under separate influences in the North and in the South. The new songs that were created on either side were not interchanged. Those which the southerners sang were in a more continuous line from the songs popular in the T'ang and Northern Sung. It is said that these finally became the nan-ch'ü that were popular at the beginning of Ming. It was only after the unification of Yüan that the southerners became acquainted with the songs of the North which, still redolent of their vulgar origins, seemed to them fresh and new and worthy of collection, something that had not, incidentally, occurred to very many northerners.

Keeping in mind the tenuous relationship between the extant material and actual verse production in history, we may consider what signs of verse development a corpus of material might show. To do this, it is best to distinguish signs of linguistic development from

---

the most part examines the evidence carefully and is also useful reading. For tracing formal links between tz'u and ch'ü, one of the best is Lu Chi-yeh, *Tz'u ch'ü yen-chiu*, pp. 85–105; and for views on the soundest approach to the study of tz'u and ch'ü, see Jen Na, *Tz'u ch'ü t'ung yi*, pp. 1–3. Both these books examine tz'u and ch'ü from the similarities of their origins rather than from their dissimilar surface features.

I have not included here works which emphasize music theory. On the other hand, none of the works above takes the pragmatic approach quite as far as Wang Li does in HYSLH. (A list of abbreviations of frequently cited works will be found in the Bibliography.)

levels of style one might discern in the corpus. The development of
language, with its phonological, lexical, and syntatic changes, pro-
ceeds more or less regularly along the scale of time, and is suitable
as a means of dating verse or verse types and as a means of distinguishing those types whose prosodic features retain the linguistic
characteristics of a previous age. Different levels of style, on the
other hand, may occur in any verse type irrespective of time and so
cannot show of themselves generic differences between the verse of
different periods. Even if we allow that extant verse represents the
most significant verse of an age, there is no justification in attempting to show the development of verse from one age to the next, as
Liu Ta-chieh and so many others have done, by comparing the literary
verse of one period to the colloquial verse of the other. It is more
reasonable to say that levels of style show much better the literary
status of a corpus of verse. For such purposes style levels may be
divided as follows:

> Folk song
> Song verse
>   Primary verse
>   Secondary verse
> Literary verse

Folk song is taken here as a prototype; it is the original song in
which words and music are combined for the first time. After the folk
song becomes known, song verse appears, and according to its direct
or indirect relationship to the folk song, it can be subdivided into
primary and secondary types. Primary song verse is the new set of
words composed to the song tune by a person who knows the folk song
and perhaps can perform it. The diction imitates the colloquial language and the techniques of verse making are spontaneous and flexible. Secondary song verse shows more influence from the literary
tradition both in theme and style and is composed by someone to whom
the song music or dialect of the original song probably is not second
nature—because of geographical location, for example, or musical
ineptitude. These writers resort to more rigid techniques of verse
making because they have recourse only to written examples, and
nuances and spontaneous turns of phrase in folk song or primary verse
have either to be imitated blindly or replaced with something easily
managed, like stereotyped phrases. It is likely that only those of
literary bent compose verse in such circumstances; the folk and un-
educated do not need to because there is always sufficient musical
material to occupy them. Literary verse, finally, has least to do with
a verse form's origins in music. It conforms to the rhythms and sym-
metries of an abstract pattern divorced from the words or music of any
particular song. Such patterns emerge through the efforts of poets or
prosodists seeking a perfect form by which to write verse.

In the light of these considerations, Yüan san-ch'ü is best described as a corpus of song verse whose pieces range from primary
verse closely related to folk song, to secondary verse closely related
to literary verse. This is true of tz'u, and with the added fact that
before the end of T'ang there was considerable literary verse in the
corpus the same can be said of *shih* 詩, the representative verse of
the T'ang dynasty. The greater formal freedom, the realism and greater
scope of themes usually considered by literary historians to be a
special characteristic of san-ch'ü, are by no means unique to the
Yüan dynasty and should be viewed as developments long since
established in colloquial verse of previous ages. Linguistic change
that took place in North China during the Liao and Chin is the soundest criterion on which to found the special characteristics of san-ch'ü.
Developments in syntax are not so easily detected, but new lexical
items as well as some change in word structure are evident. The results of phonological development, however, are clear, in that sets
of rhyme words differ from earlier times and the tones of syllables
group themselves differently, so that techniques of matching the syllable and word to the corresponding segment of music show differences that have come to the notice of prosodists. In ch'ü there was
also a greater tendency to rhyme words whose tones were different.
This to many historians sets san-ch'ü off from other verse, but again
cross-tone rhymes, like the prosodic developments described above,
are not really new but a continuation of trends noticeable much earlier.[5]
The diction of a high proportion of ch'ü does show distinct tendencies
toward the colloquial language; the adjective with doubled onomatopoeic syllables and the extrametrical syllable, both to be discussed
in detail later, are the most important of the devices that suggest this.

History and Terminology

In traditional terminology ch'ü includes both *hsi-ch'ü* 戲曲, or
songs written for the drama, and san-ch'ü which were written as individual pieces not intended for performance on stage. Except for
minor points of style, the songs of the drama and san-ch'ü are the
same. In a play the plot is revealed through dialogue interspersed
with songs; an act has its basis in the special grouping of songs according to established patterns called "sets."[6] San-ch'ü takes the
form either of *hsiao-ling* 小令 or of sets like those in the drama, but

---

5. For a discussion of cross-tone rhymes in tz'u, see Wang Li,
HYSLH, pp. 558—64. He maintains that the practice is much more restricted in tz'u than it is in ch'ü.

6. For full discussions on the form of Yüan drama, see Yoshikawa
Kojiro, *Yüan tsa-chü yen-chiu*, pp. 9—19, and Wang Ching-ch'ang,
Ch'ü hsüeh li shih, pp. 132—40.

in neither is dialogue used. Hsiao-ling refers to single songs, either folk or literary, but because Yüan music is lost, a hsiao-ling is for practical purposes the words of one verse form. Sets of songs take different forms linking from two to a dozen or more hsiao-ling into a unit. Groups of three or more are called *t'ao-shu* 套數.[7] Being written to music, the songs that were grouped together had to be in the same mode. Later, even after the music was no longer current, writers would still adhere to the conventions determining which song could and which could not be included in a particular t'ao-shu. This was not a problem for Yüan writers, of course, as their choice of songs was based on their understanding of the music.[8]

Historical records state that in North China during the Chin and Yüan dynasties the seven-tone scale came to be used in popular music, but there is no way to corroborate this as the music has not been sufficiently preserved. Our knowledge of pitch values and interval patterns in the modes is hardly better. The nine modes[9] in common use during the Yüan were called:

Huang chung	Nan lü
Cheng kung	Shuang tiao
Ta-shih tiao	Yüeh tiao
Hsien lü	Shang tiao[10]
Chung lü	

Some were more frequently used for san-ch'ü than others. If the number of surviving hsiao-ling are an indication, the modes most used were the Shuang tiao and Chung lü. Very few hsiao-ling tunes survive in the Ta-shih tiao and Huang chung modes.

The verse forms, or *ch'ü p'ai* 曲牌, that were the basis for the form of san-ch'ü verses amount in the northern ch'ü to over two hundred. Including those used in the drama, the number is usually said to exceed five hundred. The ten ch'ü p'ai with the most surviving hsiao-ling are, in descending order:

---

7. Two songs linked are called *tai-kuo* 帶過 "carry-over." Sometimes, but not often, three songs linked this way could be called tai-kuo.

8. For a more detailed discussion of these forms, see Jen Na, *San-ch'ü kai lun*, pp. 12–32; CKSCS, pp. 20–39; and Alfred Hoffman, "Kurze Einführung in die Technik der *San-ch'ü*."

9. Although T'ao Tsung-yi, *Ch'o keng lu*, xxvii, p. 415, and Chou Te-ch'ing both say there are seventeen modes, it is accepted that nine were in common use for hsiao-ling. See Wu Nan-hsün, *Lü-hsüeh huei t'ung*, pp. 292–95.

10. The modes and the verse forms mentioned here and later in the discussion are listed, with Chinese characters, in the Appendix.

1. Che kuei ling	6. Ch'ing chiang yin
2. Shui hsien-tzu	7. Tsui t'ai-p'ing
3. Hsi ch'un lai	8. Hsiao t'ao hung
4. Hung hsiu hsieh	9. P'u t'ien lo
5. Luo mei feng	10. Tien ch'ien huan

This does not necessarily show general popularity; totals from the four major Yüan anthologies give a variety of results. If one considers the number of known writers and the number of anonymous hsiao-ling for each verse form, the following order emerges which is probably nearer the popular choice:

1. Shui hsien-tzu	6. P'u t'ien lo
2. Hsi ch'un lai	7. Tien ch'ien huan
3. Che kuei ling	8. Yüeh chin ching
4. Hung hsiu hsieh	9. Ch'ing chiang yin
5. Luo mei feng	10. Wu yeh-er

Although they in no certain way tell which verse forms were most popular in the Yüan dynasty, the lists are useful when a cross-section of verse is needed to show how poetic features and rules of prosody appeared in actual practice.

Literary historians usually designate two periods in the development of san-ch'ü. The first covers most of the thirteenth century and the second extends from the beginning of the fourteenth century to the end of the Yüan dynasty (1367). The former period was called a time of minor development because, it was said, the creative energy of the talented was spent on writing the drama, while san-ch'ü was written only as a pastime. It was the second period that received the highest praise from traditional critics. To them it was the golden age when san-ch'ü was elevated to a literary form worthy of practice. Chang K'o-chiu and Ch'iao Chi, the two most outstanding writers of the period, were called the Li Po and Tu Fu of san-ch'ü.

Recent critics, however, have abandoned this viewpoint. Luo Chint'ang in his comment on the two periods writes:

> In the works of the first period, *hao-fang* 豪放 was foremost and *ch'ing-li* 清麗 secondary....[11] After the fall of the Southern Sung (1279)...there was a gradual departure from the natural style of popular literature...and a trend toward classicism. As regards literary style one can say this was an advancement, but the sincerity, the freshness of language, and the spontaneity so characteristic of the earlier period were no more to be seen. This seems to be the inevitable course of literary art. (CKSCS, 1:39)

---

11. These two terms are not readily translatable. *Hao-fang* refers to a free style in writing in which a poet would sacrifice style rather than alter the thought he wishes to express. *Ch'ing-li* refers to a more elegant style of writing.

In a more recent history of literature there is the following note on Chang K'o-chiu:

> Critics in the Ch'ing dynasty said that his [Chang K'o-chiu's] songs approached classic elegance and "never descended to the language used in the drama," and that "in the elegance of balanced phrases he advanced the technique of *yüeh-fu* [i.e., san-ch'ü]; for various lines he chose the most beautiful of the Sung and T'ang dynasties." They thought they were praising Chang K'o-chiu but instead they were only pointing out his shortcomings.[12]

It is suggested that the division into periods indicates that san-ch'ü had caught the fancy of writers with a literary bent soon after China was united under Yüan, implying once again that writers of literary style were beginning to usurp the form. The increase of literary style in the corpus at this time is probably a reflection of wider popularity among the literati, who tended to use literary style more often. Since folk song and much of primary verse are the more ephemeral, there will be a proportionately greater amount of the verse preserved which was written by the literati. A case in point is the san-ch'ü of Chang K'o-chiu, a most voluminous collection which must represent a very high percentage of his total production. Could as much be said for other writers both known and anonymous and from both the early and late periods, this question of tendency toward literary style in the second period might not have arisen.[13] As matters stand, the evidence is not complete enough to say with certainty that any one style "dominated" song verse composition in either the early or later period.

Sources

Relatively speaking the amount of san-ch'ü that has been preserved is very small.[14] Only four major anthologies have survived from Yüan times: two, the *Yang ch'un pai hsüeh* (YCPH) and the *T'ai-p'ing yüeh-fu* (TPYF), are known to have been collected by Yang Chao-ying (fl. 1300); the other two, the *Yüeh-fu hsin sheng* (YFHS) and the *Yüeh-fu ch'ün yü* (YFCY), are by unknown editors.[15] By comparing the

---

12. *Chung-kuo wen-hsüeh shih*, pp. 791−92.

13. The collected san-ch'ü of only three writers have survived; the verse of all the other authors survive in general ch'ü collections, song registers, tz'u collections, and in works not related to song verse. See CYSC, the introduction, pp. 1−2, 4.

14. Allowing proportionately for the greater duration of the T'ang and Sung, the number of Yüan san-ch'ü preserved amounts to about one-fifth the number of verses in the *Ch'üan t'ang shih* and one-half the number in the *Ch'üan sung tz'u*. For figures, see CYSC, introduction, pp. 8−9.

15. Jen Na says that the YFCY was probably edited by Hu Ts'un-shan of Yüan times. See his prefatory notes, p. 1a.

contents of the four collections, Jen Na conjectures that the YFCY is
earlier than the TPYF and that it was possibly the first anthology of
san-ch'ü (YFCY, app., pp. 8b-9a). It is a collection of hsiao-ling
only, of which there are 627. According to Jen Na, of these, 325 are
not in any of the other Yüan collections (YFCY, p. 1a). The arrangement is by authors of the songs rather than mode and verse form, as
is usually true of other collections, and it includes the work of twenty-
three writers, of seven of whom there is no record in any other source.[16]

We know the YCPH to be the earlier of Yang Chao-ying's collections. Teng Tzu-chin remarks in the preface to the TPYF: "There is
the collection, *Yang ch'un pai hsüeh*, of Yang Tan-chai [i.e., Yang
Chao-ying] which has been in circulation for a long time; now he has
recently made the present collection." The YCPH is usually in ten
chüan; the songs are arranged by mode and verse form and both hsiao-
ling and t'ao-shu are included. A nine-chüan edition, discovered and
annotated by Sui Shu-shen, contains sixty-eight hsiao-ling and six-
teen t'ao-shu not found in any other edition of the YCPH; thirty-one
of the hsiao-ling and twelve of the t'ao-shu are not to be found any-
where else.[17]

The TPYF first appeared in the middle of the fourteenth century.
This second collection of Yang Chao-ying included works of "famous
writers of the time in all walks of life which had not appeared in any
of the other anthologies" (TPYF, see Teng's preface). There are eight-
and nine-chüan editions but only the latter was available for present
reference. It includes both hsiao-ling and t'ao-shu which are also
arranged by mode and verse form.

Of the four anthologies, least is known of the background of YFHS.
It is in three chüan; the first is devoted wholly to t'ao-shu and the
second and third are given over to hsiao-ling. The arrangement is
again by mode and verse form. The texts of songs sometimes differ
considerably from those in other sources; authors of the songs are
often omitted.

Although Yüan songs are preserved in other works, both of the Yüan
dynasty and later, it is mostly from these four anthologies that the
songs to be discussed below are chosen.

Ming anthologies have preserved Yüan san-ch'ü, though the texts
often vary from those in the Yüan anthologies. Of the most useful,
the earliest are the *Sheng shih hsin sheng* and Chang Lu's revision
and expansion of it, the *Tz'u lin chai yen*. The *Yung-hsi yüeh-fu*
would be the most valuable for studies of Yüan verse except that
names of authors are not given. Another collection, *Yüeh-fu ch'ün chu*
(YFCC), suggested by Jen Na to be earlier than *Yung-hsi yüeh-fu*,
was recently recovered in a Ming copy and reprinted in a modern edi-

---

16. Jen Na, *Ch'ü hsieh*, ii, 60b.

17. See *Hsin chiao chiu chüan pen* YCPH, pp. 205—6.

tion.[18] Finally, there is the *Nan pei kung tz'u chi* of Ch'en Suo-wen
(died before 1604) in which songs of fifty-six Yüan writers, as well
as many anonymous pieces, are collected.

As for the collected san-ch'ü of individual writers, only those of
Chang K'o-chiu, Ch'iao Chi, and Chang Yang-hao[19] have survived.
All three writers are from the latter half of the Yüan dynasty. The
most readily available editions of their works are movable type editions in the *San-ch'ü ts'ung k'an* (SCTK) and *Yin hung yi suo k'o ch'ü*.
These as well as the several modern compilations of the works of a
few other writers from various earlier sources have been superceded
by the *Ch'üan yüan san-ch'ü* (see below).

There are several modern anthologies the two best of which are
Ch'en Nai-ch'ien's *Yüan jen hsiao-ling chi* (YJHLC) and Sui Shu-
shen's *Ch'üan yüan san-ch'ü* (CYSC). Ch'en's book includes the vast
majority of Yüan hsiao-ling and is arranged by verse form. Sui's book
claims to include all san-ch'ü of the Yüan period and the material in
it is arranged by author, with sources given for each verse. Except
where there is a problem concerning the text of a verse, these two
books are the source references given for all verses quoted below.

A useful book for general background is Luo Chin-t'ang's *Chung-
kuo san-ch'ü shih* (CKSCS). It contains much about history and form
and, like Cheng Chen-to's *Ch'a t'u pen chung-kuo wen-hsüeh shih*,
gives notes on the lives of san-ch'ü writers. As for general histories
of literature, the treatment of san-ch'ü in the K'o-hsüeh yüan *Chung-
kuo wen-hsüeh shih* is exceptional in that there is critical comment
which, though written with social realist bias, is usually well founded.
The best organized study of prosody is *Han-yü shih-lü hsüeh* (HYSLH),
even though Wang Li follows the song registers (ch'ü p'u 曲譜) too
unquestioningly to be able to show usage among Yüan writers. Of all
the song registers, I have found that the *Pei hsiao-ling wen-tzu p'u*
of Luo K'ang-lieh best represents practice among Yüan writers of san-
ch'ü, but Luo Chin-t'ang's *Pei ch'ü hsiao-ling p'u* is very useful also.

Wu Mei's writings on *ch'ü* are valuable because of the wealth of
knowledge of traditional background they contain. They always include, as the traditional branch of ch'ü studies does, all the current
statements about music, its relationship to the words and the manner
of performance.

The Transcription

Before san-ch'ü could be analyzed it was necessary to determine
as closely as possible what the sound of Yüan Chinese was, and to
represent it in a phonetic transcription. In the first quarter of the

---

18. *Ch'ü hsieh*, ii, p. 60.

19. Sui Shu-shen, CYSC, introduction, p. 4, adds T'ang Shih 湯式,
but though he was born in Yüan he lived most of his life under Ming.

fourteenth century Chou Te-ch'ing compiled *Chung-yüan yin-yün* (CYYY), a rhyme table for the use of versifiers who were not familiar with the dialect of the "central plain" (that is, roughly the area between the eastern part of modern Shensi and the western part of Shantung). How closely this rhyme table reflects the sounds of the northern dialect in Yüan is a matter of conjecture; however, it is the most useful tool available for reconstructing the sound system of the language used for Yüan san-ch'ü.

Yüan Chinese resembles the modern National Language more than, for example, the National Language and Cantonese resemble one another.[20] Vowel and initial consonant values appear to be close to the modern language, and in Yüan, as in modern times, final -p, -t, and -k (i.e., the entering tone 入聲) either no longer existed in the North or were evident only in vestigial form;[21] unlike the modern language, however, Yüan Chinese retained final -m. Tones were differentiated much as they are now—that is, into four classes. However, words in the entering tone of earlier times often differed in tone from the modern language.

---

20. However, see Hugh Stimson, *The Jongyuan In Yunn*, p. 10, who claims that "Old Mandarin [i.e., the Chinese of the CYYY] is not a direct ancestor of modern Pekingese, but rather stands in an uncle-nephew relationship." See also his "Phonology of the *Chung-yüan yin-yün*," pp. 132—33.

21. In two different places in his *Chung-yüan yin-yün cheng yü tso tz'u ch'i li* (the second chüan of the CYYY), Chou Te-ch'ing remarks that the entering tone was still evident in the spoken language, and its being mixed with other tones was merely to make available a greater variety of rhyme words. How exactly the entering tone was still evident in the spoken language is quite impossible to know now but its development into the other tones is more real than Chou Te-ch'ing's statement implies because it is not only evident in the rhyming of words but in the meter of lines as well. In his "Tso tz'u shih fa" ("Ten rules on writing tz'u," i.e., ch'ü), in the last section in the second chüan of CYYY, he cautions versifiers to take particular care over the entering tones that have become p'ing tones because if used as they would be in archaic prosody, they would ruin the meter of the line. It would be interesting to see how many northern writers, if any, made mistakes in meter because they felt a certain word was still in the entering tone when they should have taken it as a p'ing tone. It seems as though Chou Te-ch'ing starts with the assumption that a writer "hears" the entering tone more strongly than the new tone into which the word had changed and has to adjust to the new tone in rhyming and in the meter just as National Language speakers now must adjust for the entering tone when imitating T'ang shih. The assumption is likely to be true of southern writers, but not so likely for northern writers, to say nothing of folk singers.

Table 1. Initials

	Labial	Apical	Retracted apical	Dorsal
Voiceless				
Aspirate stops	p	t	–	k
Unaspirate stops	b	d	–	g
Aspirate affricates	–	ts	ch	–
Unaspirate affricates	–	dz	zh[1]	–
Spirants	f	s	sh	h
Voiced				
Spirants	v	–	–	–
Nasal	m	n	–	–
Retroflex	–	–	r[2]	–
Lateral	–	l	–	–
No initial	–	–	–	unmarked

1. *zh* as *j* in judge (*zh*, *ch*, and *sh*, even though they may appear before *i*, are always enunciated rather far back).

2. *r* as in raw, with tip of tongue drawn back.

In the analysis of san-ch'ü, a phonetic transcription of Yüan Chinese has to serve two purposes. On the one hand it should keep all the phonological distinctions, and on the other it should be "readable," that is, present a fair impression of the sounds and yet not require too much adjustment for English speakers.[22] Of the three parts of the syllable, the initials, are treated as shown in Table 1. The medials are given as -i-, -u-, and -iu- (that is, ü). The finals are as listed according to the nineteen rhyme groups in the *Chung-yüan yin-yün* of Chou Te-ch'ing:

1. -ung 東鍾
2. -ang 江陽
3. -r, -z 支思
4. -i, -əi 齊微
5. -u, -iu 魚模
6. -ai, -oi 皆來
7. -ən 真文
8. -an, -on 寒山
9. -uon 桓歡
10. -ien, iuen 先天
11. -au, -ao 蕭豪
12. -o 歌戈
13. -a 家麻
14. -e 車遮
15. -əng 庚青
16. -ou 尤候
17. -əm 侵尋
18. -am, -om 監咸
19. -iem 廉纖

22. In achieving this, the analysis of the CYYY by Stimson in *The Jongyuan In Yunn* has been the most help.

For our purposes it is not necessary that the transcription consistently keep the vowels and endings distinct from medials. Thus group 1 is -ung, not -uəng, group 3 is -r, not -rə, etc. In groups 7, 15, and 17 the distinguishing feature is the ending, -n, -ng, -m, respectively. The vowel, ə, is "neutral" and derives its color from vocal positioning of the initial or medial. In group 8, -on is never labialized and so is not confused with -uon of group 9, but a few graphs have either final. Within groups 3, 4, 5, 6, 8, 11, and 18 there is more than one spelling in the present transcription for finals that are considered to rhyme. These could be eliminated but because they probably represent some difference of sound and present no real problems in keeping the rhyme groups distinct, it was felt beneficial to retain them.

Table 2. Vowels

	Rounded		*Unrounded*
High	-u, -iu		-i
			-ə, -r, -z
	-ou		-e
		-o	
Low			-a

Vowels are shown in Table 2. The symbols for vowels in the transcriptions are to be read as follows:

u	as double *o* in *boot*
iu	as German *ü*
a	as in *father*
r	as double *r* in *'brr'*
z	as double *z* in *'bzz'*
i	as in *machine*
ə	as *e* in *the* when it stands first in the syllable. It is a neutral vowel of very brief duration taking color from what precedes it.
e	as in *led*
o	as *ou* in *bought*
au	as *ou* in *out*
ao	as *ou* in *out*
ou	as *o* in *note*

The four tones set out in the CYYY are called *yin-p'ing* 陰平, *yang-p'ing* 陽平, *shang* 上, and *ch'ü* 去. They are indicated in the transcriptions with diacritics —*diēm, diém, diêm, dièm*, respectively.[23]

---

23. Purely for convenience, the tone mark is always over the last vowel in the syllable and so does not necessarily indicate that one

Syllables that have developed from the entering tone have both the
diacritic indicating their new tone and a period after the syllable,
thus *de͡t.*, *ti͡e.*, etc. As their actual contour during the Yüan is uncer-
tain, tones may be read as the four tones in the National Language,
but according to Wang Li (HYSLH, p. 787) the yin-p'ing was probably
a level tone in the middle register, the yang-p'ing a rising tone in
the middle register, the shang a level tone in the upper register, and
the ch'ü a falling tone in the lower register. In this respect, Wang Li
does not agree entirely with those who base their views on a study of
singing styles that have come down from early times (see Chapter 1).
The following chart summarizes roughly both Wang Li's view and the
view of others:

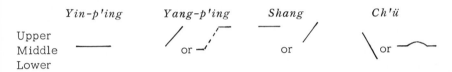

	Yin-p'ing	*Yang-p'ing*	*Shang*	*Ch'ü*
Upper				
Middle	——	or	or	or
Lower				

     To the right of each example of verse in the discussion, except in
the one or two instances otherwise stated, a metrical pattern based
on Luo K'ang-lieh's *Pei hsiao-ling wen-tzu p'u* is given for comparison with the tone patterns of the example. The notation is as follows:

p p'ing   s shang   c ch'ü   r mandatory rhyme
t tse   *s* shang or p'ing   x any tone   *r* optional rhyme

     As a matter of convenience two separate romanizations are used:
for the names of people and places, titles of books and poems, and
technical terms that are in Chinese, the Wade–Giles system is used.
For the texts, and for parts of the texts discussed separately, the
system described above is used.

The Analysis

     In the development of any nation's literature, verse analysis plays
an important part. In the past it was aimed at establishing prescrip-
tions for creating more verse. Analysis done with such aims concerned general standards of good form perhaps more than the actual
practice among writers of the verse under examination. It is the aim
of this book to attempt, through analysis, a description of the techniques and imagery that occur in san-ch'ü.
     In the analysis of poetic style, technique and imagery are at two
extremes. If taken together they help give an understanding of the
manner in which rhetorical features function to create the general

---

vowel alone carries the tone. This is especially to be remembered
when reading vowel clusters and a vowel spelled with more than one
letter.

effects of a poem. For this purpose it seems appropriate to divide
rhetorical features according to their function into three main classes
with five subgroups:

      I.   Phonological
         1. Meter
         2. Rhyme
     II. Phonological and semantic
         3. Sound color
         4. Repetition patterning
    III. Semantic
         5. Figuration

The five subgroups represent five separate aspects of analysis, though
they are actually related on a gradual scale. Thus at one extreme is
meter whose relation to semantic facets of the poem is indirect, and
on the other extreme is the figure of speech which functions primarily
in the semantic realm but whose effect is regulated by, among other
things, the amount of language needed to carry it. At the midpoint one
finds devices like parallelism and onomatopoeia in which special
meanings are derived from a more evenly balanced interplay of form
or sound with semantic elements.

As far as possible, the general practice of san-ch'ü writers has
been indicated. This was somewhat easier in technical matters, but
as semantic elements entered into the analysis it became increasingly
difficult to feel that a few concrete examples could represent general
practice. This was true especially with the discussion of speech
figures in which a system of logical possibilities was presented with
concrete examples but with little indication of how well the examples
represented usage.

The ultimate justification of descriptive analysis is its importance
to the translator who is often limited in the scope of his approach just
when he should be most free to judge the style of the pieces he translated. In the words of Paul Goodman:

> Good translation is grounded in practical formal criticism, for the
> translator must estimate just what parts are strongly functioning
> in giving the effect.... In excellent translations entire systems
> of relations are altered or neutralized in order to save certain
> parts that the translator believes to be crucial; the imagery is
> altered in order to save the rhymes and stanzas, or the rhymes
> are sacrificed in order to save the imagery; the incidents and
> references may be completely renovated in order to keep the at-
> titude of topical satire.... [24]

The translations in the text are necessarily literal rather than poetic so that points of the analysis may be the more easily followed.

---

24. Paul Goodman, *The Structure of Literature*, p. 227.

Because of this it is not always possible to show what "systems of relations" in the original would be "altered or neutralized" to make a balanced poetic translation. However, it is the aim of the discussions to indicate which of the relationships appear to have strongest and which more neutral effects in a line or in the whole poem.

Throughout the discussion the illustrative examples are nearly always quoted with full context, even when it would have been sufficient to quote only one or two lines. At times this may seem unnecessarily cumbersome but there are two reasons for it. First, although the themes of san-ch'ü are not specifically within the scope of the book, a reader can easily get a view of the subject matter treated in the genre simply by reading through the texts and translations. Second, I have found that many quotations of lines out of context lose more easily their relationship to the whole corpus and tend to become unreal, like exercise sentences in a grammar. Finally, although this book cannot lead directly to establishing the universals of style in literature, it is hoped that some of the methods of analysis either used or suggested in it will encourage further work in Chinese literature, and perhaps even in Western literature, in seeking these universals.

I

Meter

The metrical structure imposed on the language of verse is usually based upon one of the three fundamental aspects of syllable enunciation, that is, stress, duration, or pitch. Since a system of pitch variations is decisive in understanding Chinese utterance, it is only natural that the meter of Chinese verse be described in terms of pitch, as in fact it has been for the past several centuries.[1] In a line of Chinese verse the patterns which stress and duration form do not easily allow arrangement into fixed metrical structure.[2] For the same reason, it would be difficult to develop a metrical system for English verse based on the pitch of syllables, or even on the general intonation of a line, because these are so liable to vary among speakers of English.[3]

---

1. We are speaking here of the pitches themselves, which, though they differ considerably in contour from one dialect to another, are the basis for a system of tones that is standard throughout the language.

2. This is an extremely complex problem. Duration is closely bound up with pitch in Chinese poetry but not so simply as to say merely that the p'ing tone is long and the tse tone is short. For discussions of this problem, see Chou Fa-kao, "Shuo p'ing-tse," and Chou Ts'e-tsung, "Ting hsing hsin-shih t'i te t'i-yi," pp. 5—6. It can be seen that certain tone patterns yield a tendency, in a normal reading of traditional poetry, to elongate some of the p'ing tones in the line, but not much has yet been done to ascertain whether it is a particular pattern of durations that determines the pitch pattern or whether it is a certain pitch pattern that determines the durations. It is perhaps safer to assume the latter, especially in poetry written under the influence of tranditional concepts of meter.

3. For a discussion of this, see J. H. Levis, *Foundations of Chinese Musical Art*, pt. 1. In his introduction, p. 4, he refers to the

Metrical systems before the Southern Sung had only two contrasting elements, the *p'ing* 平 and *tse* 仄 tones, that distinguished a
level tone having an unchanging pitch from the three other tones,
that is, the clipped tone and the oblique tones that were either rising
or falling. Although the best shih and tz'u[4] poets may have been
more meticulous about the use of tones than the p'ing-tse system required, it was only in treatises on the metrics of san-ch'ü that the
p'ing, shang, and ch'ü tones were distinguished strictly enough to
affect the description of metrical patterns.

Because of developments in the tone system of the spoken language, the p'ing tone in the Yüan dynasty split into two types: the
yin-p'ing approximated a level tone in the middle register and the
yang-p'ing was a rising tone in the middle register (see pp. 16—17).
As the shang tone was still in the higher register, the relative pitch
and perhaps the contour as well was similar to the yang-p'ing, which
could explain why one so often sees them used interchangeably. On
the other hand, there were positions in which the yin and yang-p'ing
tones were best kept separate. In his postface to the *Chung-yüan
yin-yün*, Chou Te-ch'ing recounts the following incident:

> Fu-ch'u 復初 raised his cup; the singer was singing the popular
> song "Ssu k'uai yü," and when he reached the lines
>
> 影扇歌青樓飲
>
> tsaî shièn gō, tsiǎng loú iǎm
>
> (Luo) Tsung-hsin (羅) 宗信 stopped the song and said to me, "When
> you sing *tsaî* parallel to *tsiǎng*, *tsiǎng* becomes *tsióng* 晴. In my
> estimation of the melody, if in this position a p'ing tone is to be
> used, its pitch must be raised, but with *tsiǎng* 青 its pitch is held
> down; that makes it incorrect. (CYYY, i, p. 1a)

In the same way there were positions in which the shang and ch'ü
tones, though traditionally in one category, were seen to be no longer
compatible.[5] Again Chou Te-ch'ing writes: "*mi* 蜜 [in the verse form

---

surd-sonant scale of initial consonants as a type of "stress." I prefer at present to look on it as alliteration.

4. For a full discussion of strict patterns in tz'u, see Wang Ch'in-
hsi, "Sung tz'u shang-ch'ü-sheng tzu yü hsi-ch'ü kuan-hsi ji ssu-
sheng-t'i k'ao-cheng."

5. It is of questionable value to argue whether these fine distinctions of tones arose from new developments in the spoken language
or from changes in music. These are problems that have confronted
those in all ages who set words to music. For educated writers in a
time as late in the literary development of Chinese as the Yüan dynasty, the matter was slightly complicated by their understanding of
traditional metrics. At this point the most important development was
the critical sophistication of Chou Te-ch'ing and his friends that
allowed them to consider these points in such detail.

Hsi ch'un lai, line 1, last syllable], being a ch'ü tone, is a good
choice; in this position there definitely cannot be a shang tone. It
is important that *huòn* 喚 is a ch'ü tone but *kî* 起 [i.e., the position
in which *kî* occurs] can be either p'ing or shang [*huòn* and *kî* are the
second and last syllables of the fourth line, which is three syllables
in length]."[6]

The way in which Wu Mei in his *Ku ch'ü chu t'an* describes the
vocal delivery of tones in singing is useful here because it shows
the musical characteristics that the tone of a syllable takes when
translated into song. He states that a p'ing tone is longest in duration; its point of most stress is at the beginning, from which it tapers
off gradually. In a yin-p'ing the note is continuous and clear and
must be sung in one breath, but a yang-p'ing is in two notes, the
first of which is short and clearly separate from the second; this second note "is sung continuously in one breath until the tone is com-
pleted." The shang tone begins in the same manner as a p'ing tone
but briskly rises and does not return to the original pitch. The ch'ü
tone has an "elliptical" shape when sung; from the initial note the
pitch gradually rises and then returns to the same pitch.[7]

This is not to suggest that every syllable in a song is sung in the
above manner, but at the positions in an established metrical pattern
where a particular tone seems to be preferred it is safe to assume
that the technique of delivery Wu Mei describes is generally characteristic of the corresponding portion of melody which dominated the
metrical form of the line. If we see it is only at such points that the
melody was distinctive enough to require the use of certain tones in
the metrical pattern, it becomes easier to understand why tones were
strictly prescribed in some positions and not in others. When songs
became recited poetry, however, the metrical pattern, being the only
"music" left, dominated the line, and choice of tones became much
stricter throughout.

Before examining the tone patterns of san-ch'ü, it would be
helpful to look at Wang Li's system of measuring *chieh-tsou* 節奏
(HYSLH, pp. 75—76). He divides all lines into groups of disyllables;
thus a six-syllable line has three rhythm units, for example,

pp tt pp[8]

which are designated from right to left as the ultimate, the penulti-

---

6. CYYY, ii, p. 53b. See also Jen Na's comments in TTSFSC, pp.
58b—59a. But see Chao Ching-shen, "Chou te-ch'ing te hsiao-ling
ting-ko," pp. 137—40, in which Chao applies to Chou Te-ch'ing's
own songs these critical standards of tones.

7. Wu Mei, *Ku ch'ü chu t'an*, ii, pp. 36—39. Although it is the
k'un-ch'ü 崑曲 style that he discusses, its vocal delivery is perhaps
the closest to that in the Yüan dynasty of any we now know.

8. The letters p and t stand for the p'ing and tse tones respectively

mate, and the antepenultimate rhythm units. The extra syllable in a
normal line with five or seven syllables stands alone as the ultimate
rhythm unit of the line; thus a five-syllable line is divided:

pp tt p

Normally a seven-syllable line is merely five syllables with a "head"
rhythm unit added at the front. In the same manner the six-syllable
line can be thought of as four syllables with another rhythm unit,
added also at the front. The fundamental difference between the odd
and even lines, therefore, is that the caesura in an odd line will always be followed by an odd number of syllables, usually three, and
the caesura in an even line by an even number of syllables, most
often four.

In regular poetry this would be a somewhat useless observation
but because syllables may be added quite freely to a line in san-ch'ü,
the position of the caesura can at times become a problem. If, as is
often the case, a line of seven syllables is actually only a six-syllable line with one syllable added at the beginning, it would be incorrect to place the caesura after the fourth syllable as in the normal
seven-syllable line. It would be

t pp tt pp *or* tpp ttpp

but never

tppt tpp

In this type of seven-syllable line the caesura corresponds with a
natural break in the six-syllable line. Therefore, although it has
seven syllables it has the rhythmic characteristics of a line with six
syllables. Because these rhythm patterns were determined by obvious
patterns in the music, it is natural that they were observed consistently by writers of song verse though they might be ignored by writers
of literary verse.

To illustrate briefly the freedom with which tones might be used in
practice I have set out below the tone patterns of the first two lines
from ten poems in the verse form Hung hsiu hsieh:[9]

Example 1

a 老夫人寛洪海量

(laû) fū riǎn kuōn húng hoî liàng   pq pq sc[10]

---

9. These are from the ten anonymous Hung hsiu hsieh in the *Hsin
chiao chiu chüan pen* YCPH, pp. 81–83; but see also YJHLC, pp. 64–
65, and CYSC, pp. 1692–93. Both of the latter include a song that is
not in the above edition of the YCPH.

10. For the analysis of these ten examples the yang-p'ing is indicated with a q to distinguish it from the yin-p'ing. The shang and
ch'ü tones are s and c. Italic *s* indicates that either p'ing or shang
is allowed but not ch'ü.

b 去筵席留下梅香

    (kiù) ién sí. lioú hà məí hiāng   qq qc qp

Example 2

a 招招拈拈寒賤

    taū taū niên niên hón dzièn   pp ss qc

b 偷偷抹抹因緣

    toū toū muô muô iən iuén[11]   pp ss pq

Example 3

a 背地裏些兒歡笑

    bəì dì (lî) siē ŕ huōn siaù   cc pq pc

b 手指兒何曾湯著

    shioû zhŕ (ŕ) hó tsáng táng zhiaú.   ss qq qq

Example 4

a 不甫能尋得箇題目

    (bû.) fû néng siə́m dəî. (go) tî mù.   sq qs qc

b 點銀燈推看文書

    (diêm) iən dōng chuəī kàn vén shiū   pp pc qp

Example 5

a 手約開紅羅帳

    shioû iò. koī húng luó zhiàng   sc pq qc

b 款擡身擦下牙牀

    (kuôn) taí shiən tsâ. hà á chuāng   qp sc qp

Example 6

a 款款的分開羅帳

    kuôn kuôn (di.) fōn koī luó zhiàng   ss pp qc

b 輕輕的擦下牙牀

    kiōng kiōng (di.) tsâ. hà á chuáng   pp sc qq

Example 7

a 雖是間阻了咱十朝五夜

    (suəī shř) gàn zhû (liau dzá) shí. zhiaū û iè   cs qp sc

b 你根前没半米兒心別

    (nî) gēn tsién (mù.) buòn mî (ŕ) siəm bié.   pq cs pq

Example 8

a 結斜裏焦天撇地

    giê. sié (lî) zhiaū tiēn piê. dì   sq pp sc

---

11. Given with *ién* in CYYY, probably a mistake.

b 橫枝兒苦眼鋪眉

héng zhī (ŕ) shiəm ân pū məí   qp ps pq

Example 9

a 背地裏些兒歡愛

bəì dì (lî) siē ŕ huôn oì   cc pq pc

b 對人前怎敢明白

(duəì) riən tsién dzâm gôm miáng baí.   qq ss qq

Example 10

a 小妮子頑涎不退

(siaû) ní dzẑ uón sién bû. tuəì   qs qq sc

b 老敲才飽病莫醫

(laû) kaū tsaí baû bièng muò. ī   pq sc cp

It is possible, ignoring exceptions and the poets' liberties, to reduce these lines to a pair of highly regular patterns:

a) tt pp tt   b) pp tt pp

A writer skilled in shih composition would be likely to see these patterns behind the lines, and in any imitation he made he would strive
to fit his language to them. If we look more closely at the tones,
noting which occur most frequently in each position of the line, we
can formulate a pattern that shows the strictest as well as the freest
position in these twenty lines. Such a pattern can be represented:

a) xx pq sc   b) pp xt qq[12]

Only the last syllable, or rhyme position, in either line is fully consistent; in the a-lines it is a ch'ü tone and in the b-lines a p'ing
tone. Moving toward the head of the line, the first syllable of the
ultimate foot in the a-lines is definitely a position in which the shang
and the yang-p'ing are interchangeable; a yin-p'ing sometimes is
used as well. In the b-lines this position most often is a yang-p'ing
tone. The ch'ü tone in example 10, line b, is exceptional. For both
syllables of the penultimate foot in the a-lines a p'ing tone is preferred, but a shang may be used even though it would appear from our
examples that a shang tone is exceptional all three times it occurs
in this foot, which are in the a-lines of examples 2 and 4. It is interesting also that when the final syllable of this foot is a shang
tone the initial syllable of the ultimate foot is, at least in these examples, always a p'ing rather than a shang. In the b-lines the final
syllable of the penultimate foot falls easily into the tse category;
the p'ing tone in line b, example 3, is exceptional. The initial syllable, however, seems to allow any tone. Both syllables of the ante-

---

12. The letter x allows any tone.

penultimate foot in the a-lines are quite free but in the b-lines they
are p'ing tones, 3b again being an exception. There are no cases in
these examples in which the yin- and yang-p'ing are incompatible.

As Yüan music is no longer extant, this is perhaps the best way in
which to judge a poet's treatment of the tones in verse. The patterns
given in most registers of ch'ü verse forms are usually prescriptive
and make no attempt to show what tendencies there were among writers
to alter tones, or what latitudes they allowed themselves with various
lines. One can see quite quickly what criteria the editors of ch'ü
registers used by comparing them with several examples from the
same verse form in the *Yüan jen hsiao-ling chi*. To illustrate, three
registers give metrical patterns for the above ten pairs as follows:[13]

Li Yü	Wang Li	Luo K'ang-lieh
a) ttt pppc	a) *pp*t tppc *or pt* tp pc	a) xt xp xt
b) ptt ptpp	b) tpp ttpp *or pp* tt pp	b) xp xt pp

Judging only on the basis of our ten examples, it would appear that
Luo K'ang-lieh's analysis is closest to normal practice, though he
should probably have specified a ch'ü tone in the rhyme position in
the a-line as the other two registers did. It is understandable that
his pattern more closely approximates ours because he concerns himself only with hsiao-ling, as we necessarily do, whereas both Wang
Li and Li Yü consider examples from the drama, which usually have
looser form. It was accepted practice among makers of traditional
song registers, as with Li Yü, to describe metrical form in terms of a
single example they felt was best, adding sometimes several other
examples to show alternate forms. Li Yü's description of the first
two lines of the Hung hsiu hsieh is not incompatible with the general
metrical structure of the lines, but to take it as an absolute standard
would be incorrect, nor was this necessarily Li Yü's intention. None
of the registers shows the nature of the initial syllable in the ultimate foot of the a-line. It is not a p'ing tone as Li Yü and Wang Li
suggest, nor is it so free as Luo K'ang-lieh implies. However, the
freedom of the initial syllables in the penult and antepenult of either
line, as Luo K'ang-lieh sees it, probably represents actual practice
better than the ten examples.

From the examples, we may make a general statement on the strictness of positions that can hold more or less for any line. We have
seen that only in the rhyme positions are the tones fixed; following
that, in order of strictness, is the final syllable in all rhythm units.
Freer still are syllables in the initial positions of rhythm units and

---

13. Li Yü, *Yi li an pei tz'u kuang cheng p'u*, see Chung lü mode,
p. 11b. Wang Li, HYSLH, p. 810. Luo K'ang-lieh, *Pei hsiao-ling wen-
tzu p'u*, p. 47. Italics mean either p'ing or tse may be used.

syllables generally nearer the beginning of the line. When comparing texts as we did above it is not always possible to know whether a metrical pattern was strict entirely because of the song tune or because of traditional considerations of meter which came to dominate because most of the surviving texts were composed as sequels to an original set of words in the manner of secondary or literary verse.

There was one point in every song where a good writer allegedly paid strict attention to tones; that was the *wu-t'ou* 務頭. From all accounts this was a form of musical climax or point of melodic beauty that a writer with a good feeling for the song would reflect in his text. Chou Te-ch'ing pointed out that if one knew the position of the wu-t'ou in a particular tune, elegant language could be used with it to achieve effects of special beauty.[14] Except where Chou Te-ch'ing indicates it in his critical notes, the positions of the wu-t'ou are no longer clear. For purposes of analysis, where tone combinations like ch'ü-shang, ch'ü-p'ing, shang-p'ing, ch'ü-shang-p'ing, etc., appear to be obligatory in the metrical patterns we can assume that the melody of the song was most attractive and that it was at such places the "elegant language" was to have been used (TTSFSC, pp. 24a—b).

In the opposite extreme, we might wonder how an author could allow himself the freedom that we see in example 3 above. Comparing it with the standard pattern,

> Standard: a) xx pq sc   b) pp xt qq
> Example 3:   a) cc pq pc   b) ss qq qq

we find the first line acceptable, but in the second line the tones of the penult and antepenult are reversed. If in the other examples the second line had indicated a particularly free use of tones, this line in example 3 might have been judged acceptable as well. This disregard for tonal pattern may be owing to the fact that *shioŭ zhř*, and *hó tsóng*, being colloquial expressions, can stand a certain amount of tonal manipulation before being rendered unrecognizable. Considering that these are not words that attract attention because of their weightiness or special beauty, it is easy to see how the author could use them in spite of a conflict between their tones and the melody. Naturally this would not be accepted by traditional critics, but with-

---

14. CYYY, ii, p. 47b. Jen Na, TTSFSC, pp. 23a—32b, gives a most useful resumé of previous critical discussion on this point, to which he adds: "It is obvious that wu-t'ou was at first purely a matter of the music and not the text. . . . It is also clear that from being an aspect of music, wu-t'ou gradually became a literary feature. Chou Te-ch'ing's statement about 'using elegant language' means that beauty of melody and beauty of language must, being brought together, produce the most brilliant effect; they must not be used separately for it would detract from the effect of both." (pp. 23a—b)

out hearing the song as it was sung originally we could not, merely on the basis of the abstract form, call these lines poor song verse.

San-ch'ü is noted for the freedom with which its lines can be expanded. The syllables added to a line beyond those required in the metrical pattern are most frequently referred to as *ch'en-tzu* 襯字 ("extrametrical syllables"), and they are not counted as part of the metrical pattern. Usually they are grammatical particles or colloquial expressions whose omission from the line affects the sense only very little. They may occur in almost any position but are generally found at the beginning of a line.[15] The ten examples above illustrate well the general distribution of extrametrical syllables. The most common type appears in example 6:

a 款款的分開羅帳

kuôn kuôn (di.) fān koǐ luó zhiàng   ss pp qc

b 輕輕的擦下牙牀

kiāng kiāng (di.) tsâ. hà á chuáng   pp sc qq

The syllable *di.* in either line is not counted in the metrical scheme and when sung it was most likely given no stress and very little duration. It is for this reason that the question of tone does not arise so clearly for extrametrical syllables. Here we can be fairly certain that a reading of *di.* in a normal recitation is similar to the manner in which it was originally sung.

There are cases in which it becomes necessary to compare the line with a standard metrical pattern before the extrametrical syllables are revealed. In example 3, for instance,

a 背地裏些兒歡笑

beǐ dì (lǐ) siē ŕ huōn siaù   cc pq pc

the syllable *ŕ*, although a noun suffix, has a position in the metrical pattern and must have been sung in the manner of a word with full meaning. A natural recitation of this line emphasizes *huōn* and *siaù*, but if we read the line to scan as a regular six-syllable line, *ŕ* gets much more of the emphasis. The only alternative would be to have sung *siē* with the duration, i.e., the portion of melody, allowed for both the third and fourth syllables, in which case *ŕ* would have been like *di.* in example 6. This, however, is unlikely; the syllable *ŕ* has the function here of filling out the line.

In many lines the ch'en-tzu are quite difficult to determine. We could arrange the following line (see p. 78), for example, in several ways:

---

15. For a useful discussion of extrametrical syllables, see HYSLH, pp. 715—29.

笑吟吟先倒在牙牀上

siaù iǎm iǎm siēn daû dzaî à chuáng shiàng   xpxtppt
(siaù iǎm) "   "   "   "   "   "   "   "
    "   (iǎm iǎm) "   "   "   "   "   "   "
    "   "   (iǎm) "   "   (dzaî)"   "   "   "

Without recourse to the music it is difficult to say which represents
best the rhythm with which the line was sung; as for recitation, the
last seems to be best.

It would appear also that an extrametrical syllable may sometimes
have been used to make a word fit better into the tune of a song. If
the melody for a certain part of a line were mi sol, for example, it is
likely that in such a position a yang-p'ing syllable would sound most
natural; in other words, a syllable of any other tone would tend to
sound like yang-p'ing and might result in some confusion. If, therefore, a poet found that the word he wanted to use was in the ch'ü tone,
he might, if it were a noun, add the suffix ŕ 兒; he could then sing
the ch'ü tone syllable on the lower pitch and let the suffix occupy the
higher pitch; thus the noun when sung would remain nearer its normal
tonal characteristics. In the last line of Kuan Han-ch'ing's Huang
chung wei quoted below, the noun lù "path" appears to be helped by
its suffix in this way:

不向煙花路兒上走

bû. hiàng iēn huā lù (ŕ) shiàng dzoû   ttppcs

Without the suffix, the syllable lù might sound like lú (or liú) which
means "donkey." Obviously not many extrametrical syllables function in this manner nor indeed does the extrametrical ŕ often function
this way.[16]

In the case of a line expanded to extremes through the use of extrametrical syllables, it might appear that all relationship to the normal rhythm would be lost. Usually, however, the rhythmic breaks fall
in the correct places and the line scans either with the original or
with a similar rhythm pattern, depending on the extent of the expansion. Line a of example 7 is a less extreme example:

a 雖是間阻了咱十朝五夜

(suəī shî) gàn zhû (liau dzá) shî. zhiaū û iè   cs qp sc

Without the extrametrical syllables, it reads:

間阻十朝五夜

gàn zhû shî. zhiaū û iè   cs qp sc

---

16. For other examples, see pp. 111, 116.

The extrametrical syllables, all concentrated in the antepenult, were undoubtedly sung very briskly. If the rhythm units were strictly observed, the four final syllables in the line were probably delivered in the normal manner. This is not necessarily how the line is recited now but the example shows the rhythmic effects that may have accounted for novelty in the original presentation of the song.

The effects to be achieved through the use of extrametrical syllables were many, and in general they were appreciated by the writers adept in the colloquial style. Writers who closely observed the standard metrical patterns of a verse form used a language that tended to be closer to the poetic tradition. On the other hand, when a poem was written with less conscious attention to form, and when the writer took greater advantage of the vocabulary and rhythms of the colloquial language, there was often a natural increase in the number of extrametrical syllables. The two following poems are in the same verse form, P'u t'ien lo, but treatment of the meter is entirely different, each achieving its proper effect. Chao Shan-ch'ing's poem has a poetic dignity and a serenity about it that comes not only from the meanings of its words but also from the static syntax and the smooth way in which it fits the verse form. In the prostitute's song, however, the torrent of words and the abundant colloquialisms strike us first and are what make her anger vivid and her disappointment believable:

Chao Shan-ch'ing (fl. 1320): Chung lü, P'u t'ien lo, "Chiang-t'ou ch'iu hsing, An Autumn Walk on the River Bank" (YJHLC, p. 78; CYSC, pp. 740–41)

1a   稻粱肥
     daù liáng fəí   tpp   *r*[17]
     The corn is fat,

 b   蒹葭秀
     giēm gā sioù   ppt   r
     The rushes tall;

2a   黃添籬落
     huáng tiēm lí luò.   xpxt *r*
     More yellow is on the hedge.

 b   綠淡汀洲
     liù. dàm tiāng zhioū   xtxp r
     Fainter green on the sandbar.

----

17. r marks mandatory rhyme; when italicized, it means rhyme is optional and it is given only when the poet chose to use rhyme. The metrical patterns given at the right are based on, but are not identical with Luo K'ang-lieh and are a standard to which the true pattern actually used in the song may be compared.

3a 木葉空
    mù. iè. kūng   xtp *r*
    Tree leaves are gone,

 b 山容瘦
    shān iúng shoù   ppt r
    The mountain's face looks thin;

4a 沙鳥翻風知潮候
    shā niaû fān fūng zhī chiaú hoù   xtpp ppt r
    The sand birds hovering in the wind know the tides,

 b 望煙江萬頃沉秋
    vàng iēn gǐang vàn kǐang chiém tsioū   tpp xtpp r
    Before one's eyes, the misty river, ten thousand
        acres of heavy autumn.

5a 半干落日
    buòn gōn luò. rì.   xptx *r*
    But half a rod more and the sun will be down,

 b 一聲過雁
    î. shiǎng guò àn   xptx *r*
    With a single cry the wild goose is gone,

 c 幾處危樓
    gî chiù uǎi loú   xtpp r
    Here and there a tall house rises steep in the air.

Anonymous: Chung lü, P'u t'ien lo, no title. (YJHLC, pp. 83–84)[18]

1a 兩三日不來家
    (liǎng sām rì.) bû. lái gā   tpp *r*
    (I thought when) he hadn't been there for two or three
        days,

 b 入門來猶咱罵
    (rì. mén laî) ioú dzá[19] mà   ppt r
    When he walks in the door I'll really bawl him out!

2a 走將來便口兒裏哩哩喇喇
    (dzoû dziāng laí bièn koû f lî) lī lī là là   xpxt *r*
    He'll come over to me, full of excuses,

 b 吃的來無上下稷稷答答
    (chî. dî. laí vú shiàng hà) dzî. dzî. dâ. dâ.   xtxp r
    Spluttering, making no sense, stuttering;

18. Not included with anonymous songs in CYSC.

19. *ioú dzá*—probably for *ioú dzz* 猶自.

3a 略性子用心機怎捉拿
(liò. sìng dzẑ iùng siə̄m gī) dzə̂m zhaô ná   xtp *r*
The slippery devil will try to worm out of it,
   how can anyone trap him!

b 涎眼腦巧待詔也難描畫
(sién ân naû kaû daǐ zhiaù iê) nán miaú huà   ppt r
I can't describe how I long for him to ask for
   my favours;

4a 割捨了我咬着牙狠一會兒和他罷
gô. shiê (liau, uô) gaō (zhio.) á (hə̂n î. huəǐ ŕ)
   húo tā bà   xtpp ppt r
But I'll put him out of mind, and when I've got
   over it, I'll tell him we're through.[20]

b 罷則罷他害羞也顛倒做了真假
(bà dzaî. bà, tā) hoǐ sioū iê diə̄n daû (dzù liau)
   zhiə̄n gâ   tpp xtpp r
If we're through, we're through, but even if he's
   sorry I won't be able to tell whether he really
   means it.[21]

5a 他猛可裏便走將來問一聲我好麼
(tā mûng kô lî bièn dzoû dziāng laǐ vèn) î. shiə̄ng
   (uô) haô mā   xptx r
But then he boldly came up and asked me how I'd
   been,

b 我只索陪着笑忍着氣怕他怒發
(uô zhî̌ suô pəǐ zhio. siaù riə̄n zhio. kǐ) pà tā nù fâ.   xptx r
And all I could do was smile back, keep in my
   temper for fear he'd get angry,

c 一兩日不來家覓一箇人去尋他
(î. liǎng rî. bû. lái gā mî̌ î. gò) rián kiù siə́m tā[22]   xtpp r
So when he leaves and doesn't come back again for
   a couple of days, I'll be looking for someone to
   go and hunt him up.

The attitude toward subject matter and the manner of setting it to
words are at opposite extremes in these poems. We can be quite

---

20. *gaō zhio. á hə̂n î. huəǐ ŕ* "clenching my teeth in resentment."
21. *diə̄n daû zhiə̄n gâ* "to turn truth and falsehood upsidedown,"
"to pull the wool over someone's eyes."
22. The reading *tā* is not given in CYYY; the character is listed
under the -*o* rhymes and is read *tuō*. For the sake of consistency I
read *tā* throughout this poem. *tā* must have been a common reading
in certain areas of China in the Yüan dynasty.

certain that the second song was clearly understood and enjoyed by
the illiterate, but to appreciate Chao's song fully a listener would
undoubtedly have needed a certain literary background. It was considered bad form to use too many extrametrical syllables,[23] but obviously this was a judgment made with a rather limited view of verse
in mind and one which did not condone use of the colloquial language
or roughness of meter.

Some san-ch'ü writers made use of contrasting free and strict
meters to develop particular effects. A group of four *tao ch'ing* 道情,
or Taoist, poems by Teng Yü-pin gives an excellent illustration of
this. The first three all show the responsibilities of life in a bad
light, insisting cynically that no matter how hard one strives, one's
efforts are bound to come to nothing. The rhythm of the lines is ir-
regular and the language fresh and vigorous. Because this gives the
poems spontaneity, one cannot help feeling that the poet was writing
with sincerity about matters close to him. In the last poem, however,
Teng Yü-pin, with quite regular meters, brings in all the clichés of
the tao ch'ing style, expressing idealistic escape from society and
the ideal contentment that it provides. This is no less sincere than
the first three poems but it is clear that the focus is on an ideal and
not necessarily on the writer's own experience. The poetic effect is
very successful. To illustrate, I quote the second and last poems
below:

Teng Yü-pin (fl. 1294): Cheng kung, Tao-tao ling, "Tao ch'ing, Taoist
Song." (YJHLC, pp. 7–8; CYSC, pp. 303–4)

The second poem:

la 一個空皮囊包裹着千重氣
(î. go kūng) pí náng baū guô (zhio.) tsiēn chúng
kì   xpxtppc r
An empty skin sack filled with ambition,

b 一個乾骷髏頂戴着十分罪
(î. go gān) kū loú diêng daì (zhio.) shŕ. fēn dzuəì   xpxtppc r
A dried skull heaped with blame;

c 為兒女使盡些拖刀計
(uəì) ŕ niû shŕ dziàn (siē) tuō daū gì   xpxtppc r
For daughters and sons I've schemed all I can,

d 為家私費盡些擔山力
(uəì) gā sẑ fəì dziàn (siē) dām shān lì.   xpxtppc r
And used up my strength for the family's fortune.

_____

23. CYYY, ii, pp. 46b–47a. For similar comment by later critics,
see TTSFSC, pp. 15b–20b.

2a 您省的也麼哥[24]

niâm siâng (di.) iê mā gō   xxtpp

Do you understand this?

b 您省的也麼哥

niâm siâng (di.) iê mā gō   xxtpp

Do you see it at all?

3 這一個長生道理何人會

(zhiê î. go) chiáng shōng daù lî hó riэ́n huэì   xpxtppc r

Who really knows how to be an immortal?

The fourth poem:

1a 白雲深處青山下

baî. iuэ̄n shiэ̄m chiù tsiēng shān hà   xpxtppc r

Deep among white clouds in green mountains,

b 茅菴草舍無冬夏

maú ām tsaû shiè vú dūng hà   xpxtppc r

A thatched and humble dwelling with neither
    winter nor summer;

c 閒來幾句漁樵話

hán laí gî giù iú tsiaó huà   xpxtppc r

In leisure I can talk with simple folk,

d 困來一枕胡盧架

kuэ̀n laí î. zhiэ̄m hú lú gà   xpxtppc r

When tired, sleep under the gourd-vine trellis;

2a 您省的也麼哥

niâm siâng (di.) iê mā gō   xxtpp

Do you understand this?

b 您省的也麼哥

niâm siâng (di.) iê mā gō   xxtpp

Do you see it at all?

3 煞強如風波千丈擔驚怕

(shaî kiáng riú) fūng buō tsiēn zhiàng dām
    giэ̀ng pà   xpxtppc r

It's better than bearing fear in a world of strife.

One's attention is drawn here also to the contrast in syntax of the
fourth poem. The second poem's lines are characterized by firm
subject-verb-object relationships while in the fourth poem the action

---

24. YJHLC has 你. See also note in CYSC, p. 303.

is merely implied, as is often the case in more "poetic" style, by the juxtaposition of certain nouns or noun phrases. Only in the last line is the action clearly expressed.

It is not always the grammatical particle or parenthetical expression that is used as an extrametrical syllable, for there was no rule stating that a noun, verb, or similar word that had a basic function in the syntax of the line could not appear in extrametrical positions. A writer of the Yüan dynasty would not have given this much thought; it was only after san-ch'ü was no longer sung that the "sense-stress" given in recitation set this syntactically functional type of extrametrical syllable apart from the weaker type. The syllables that were found to be in excess of the "normal" verse form were called *tseng-tzu* 增字 ("added words"). It became impossible in some cases to distinguish tseng-tzu from the basic text, so they often were taken as part of the original metrical pattern. This perhaps accounts for the many alternate verse forms in the song registers of later times. We have already seen that Wang Li described the lines in our ten examples above as seven syllables with the note that they "can be six syllables" (HYSLH, p. 810). In the *Pei tz'u kuang cheng p'u*, only a seven-syllable pattern was given, which shows the preference in the song registers for the seven-syllable line, and possibly indicates the frequency with which it occurred in practice. The reason for such common use of seven syllables must mean that one syllable, whether grammatically forceful or not, made little difference in the rhythm so long as the caesura was observed. Therefore, as far as the musical structure was concerned, an alternate of this type is a fiction because such minor changes in a text did not constitute a change in the music. Not all variant forms are fictions, however. Unfortunately we have no way of explaining them unless early music can be recovered or until more thorough comparative studies of the san-ch'ü can be made.

A case in point is the verse form Che kuei ling. Wang Li lists five variant forms, which may be arranged as five "sentences" in nine to twelve lines.[25] These are shown in Table 3. Although not the most popular version of this song, the most condensed is given first to show how the lines develop:[26]

---

25. HYSLH, pp. 813–14. But see Luo K'ang-lieh, pp. 103–4, who points out rightly that there can be as many as seventeen lines; for hsiao-ling, however, I have most often found ten to twelve.

26. Line 3b should probably be pptt; it is probably a typographical error in HYSLH, as in Wang Li's notation it is merely the difference between an upper and lower case of the letter representing a type of metrical pattern. See songs in this form quoted later where I use Luo K'ang-lieh's analysis.

Table 3. Varieties of Che kuei ling

	A	B	C	D	E	Rhyme
1	ppttpp	tpp ttpp	-	-	-	r
2a)	ttpp	-	-	-	-	-
b)	ttpp	-	-	-	-	r
3a)	ttpp	ttpp	ttpp	ttp	ttpp	-
b)	ttpp	pptt pp	tpp ttpp	tpp	ttpp	-
c)	-	-	-	ttpp	ttpp	r
4a)	ttpptt	ptt pptt	-	-	-	r
b)	ppttpp	tpp ttpp	tpp tttpp	-	-	r
5a)	ttpp	ttpp	ttpp	-	-	r
b)	ttpp	ttpp	ttpp	-	-	r
c)	-	ttpp	ttpp	-	-	r
d)	-	-	ttpp	-	-	r

Writers most often used versions C or D of the third sentence; in the fourth and fifth sentences version B is most frequently seen. Version B of lines 1 and 4a are again only a case of adding a syllable at the beginning of the basic line; even line 4b of version C simply has a syllable added before the antepenultimate and penultimate rhythm units. The third sentence, becoming three lines in some versions, is slightly more complicated but it is still easy to see how line 3b in version C, tpp ttpp, develops into the two lines 3b and 3c of version D, tpp and ttpp, which would have been a simple matter of syntax. It is somewhat more difficult to see how the fifth sentence was expanded to twice its normal length or, as often happens in the drama, to more than three times its normal length. It may have been possible for a Chinese singer to slow down the tempo so that the time between beats was much longer, or there may customarily have been only one or two notes per beat in the melody; he then would have been able to add several extra words and still not alter the speed of delivery beyond practicability. On the other hand, as appears to be true here since each line is rhymed and stands in some form of parallelism, the music of lines 5a and 5b may merely have been repeated for the extra lines 5c and 5d.

It is also interesting that mandatory rhyme occurs in this song only at the ends of sentences, the fifth excepted, no matter how expanded they may be. This gives indications, at least in this song form, of the melody's influence on sentence length and on the metrical system—which brings us to certain basic questions. Why is it, in a song like the Che kuei ling, most of whose lines can be doubled in length, that there are lines like 2a and 2b which rarely if ever are anything but the basic four syllables? This leads us in turn to the broader question: What exactly is the nature of the influence melody can exert upon the metrical structure of a whole piece? Unanswerable without more examination, these questions force us at least to

consider certain facts which allow a more realistic critical view of
meter. It becomes easier to see that the writer who knew the melody
of the pieces he wrote could successfully take liberties with the
verse form that others who worked only with an abstract pattern could
hardly be expected to understand. The melody is a freely flowing pattern. It is intricate in the demands it makes on the line, yet it is
easily remembered and can be followed with hardly a thought to its
complexities. It is a complete entity that can be comprehended all
at once in the mind and so its artistic structure is constantly before
the author as he writes. In the hands of a skillful versifier the balance and climax of the melodic structure develop naturally in the text
of his verse. It is this that accounts on the one hand for the success
as poems of certain pieces less elegant in diction and line, and on
the other hand for the failure of certain others in which there may be
isolated masterful lines.

The variations we have seen in the Che kuei ling are typical of
those appearing in other verse forms. There are, however, those that
can be even more radically changed as, for example, the hundred-word
Che kuei ling. It is basically the same as the twelve-line version
except that it is greatly expanded with extrametrical syllables. How
this is achieved in relation to the music is again only a matter of
conjecture, but it may be useful to examine one such expanded song,
a good illustration of which is the final song of Kuan Han-ch'ing's
t'ao-shu "The Refusal to Get Old." For the sake of continuity I have
included the first of the four songs as well:

Kuan Han-ch'ing (ca. 1220–ca. 1300): Nan lü, Yi chih hua, "Han-
ch'ing pu fu lao, The Refusal to Get Old." (CYSC, pp. 172–73)[27]

Yi chih hua:

1a 攀出牆朵朵花

    (pān) chiû. tsiáng duô duô huā   pptp

    I've plucked every flower that grows over the wall,

b   折臨路枝枝柳

    (zhiê.) liám lù zhr̄ zhr̄ lioû   ttppt r

    And gathered every willow overhanging the road[28]

---

27. The text of the Huang chung wei is according to the *Ts'ai
pi ch'ing tz'u*, v, as quoted by Cheng Chen-to, *Chung-kuo su-wen
hsüeh shih*, pp. 168–69, and CKSCS, p. 42; but see Wu Hsiao-ling,
Kuan han-ch'ing hsi-ch'ü chi, p. 952, nn. 20–22, and CYSC, p. 173n.
The *Ts'ai pi ch'ing tz'u* is not available to me.

28. Flowers and willows refer throughout the poem to courtesans.
In the two songs not quoted here Kuan Han-ch'ing lists his talents in
defense of his feeling that, though old, he still has qualities the
young cannot emulate.

2a 花攀紅蕊嫩
huā pān húng ruəî nuə̀n   ppptt
The tenderest buds were the flowers I picked;

b 柳折翠條柔
lioû zhiê. tsuəî tiaó rioú   tttpp r
And the willows I gathered, of the supplest green
    fronds;

3a 浪子風流
làng dzẑ fūng lioú   ttpp r
A wastrel, gay and dashing,

b 憑着我折柳攀花手
(piáng zhio. uô) zhiê. lioû pān huā shioû   ttppt r
Trusting to my willow gathering, flower plucking hand,

c 直熬得花殘柳敗休
(zhí. aó dəi.) huā tsán lioû baî hioū   ppttp r
I kept at it till the flowers fell and the willows
    withered;

4a 半生來折柳攀花
buòn shēng laí zhiê. lioû pān huā   tpp ttpp
Half my life I've been willow gathering and
    flower plucking

b 一世裏眠花臥柳
î. shî̀ lî mién huā uð lioû   ttt ppts r
And for a whole generation slept with flowers
    and lain among the willows.

Huang chung wei:

1 我却是
(uô kið. shî̀)
But I am an
蒸不爛煮不熟
(zhiāng bû. làn, zhiû bû. shiú.)
un-steam-soft-able, un-boil-through-able
搥不匾炒不爆
(chuəî bû. biên, chiaū bû. baù)
un-pound-flat-able, un-bake-dry-able
響璫璫一粒銅豌豆
hiâng dāng (dāng) î. lî̀. túng uōn doù   *p*p*t*t ppt r
rattling plunkety-plung coppery old bean.[29]

---

29. *túng uōn doù*, lit. "copper garden pea," —Yüan slang for a
libertine who is somewhat past his prime.

2 您子弟誰教鑽入他
(niêm dẑ dì shuəí gaù dzuōn rì. tuō)
Who said you young gentlemen could intrude
   upon her
鋤不斷斫不下
(chú bû. duòn, zhiaû. bû. hà)
un-hoe-up-able, un-cut-down-able,
解不開頓不脫
(gaî bû. koī, duàn bû. tuô.)
un-disentwine-able, un-cast-off-able,
慢騰騰千層錦套頭
màn tōng (tōng) tsiēn tsǎng giǎm taù toú   *t*tpp ttp r
intricate, thousand-fold brocade snare?[30]

3a 我翫的是梁園月
(uô uòn di. shǐ) liáng iuén iuè.   ppt
As for me, I can take pleasure in the Liang-yüan
   moon,
欽的是東京酒
(iǎm di. shǐ) dūng giǎng dzioû   *pp*t r
Drink no less than East Capital wine,

b 賞的是洛陽花
(shiâng di. shǐ) luò. iáng huā   tpp
enjoy the flowers of Lo-yang,
攀的是章臺柳
(pān di. shǐ) zhiāng tái lioû   ppt r
and pluck the willow of Chang-t'ai.[31]

4a 我也會吟詩會篆籀
(uô iê) huəí iǎm shī, huəí zhiuèn zhioû   tpp ttt r
Besides, I can compose poems, write ancient script,

b 會彈絲會品竹
huəí tán sž, huəí piǎn zhioû.   *t*pp ttt r
Play the lute and play the flute;

---

30. *giǎm taò toú*, "the brocade snare"—i.e., a courtesan's methods
of getting a man into her clutches. *taò* does not occur in CYYY.

31. Liang-yüan was a vast park made in Han times by Prince
Hsiao of Liang 梁孝王, suggesting here sophisticated tastes. The
Eastern Capital, i.e., Lo-yang, was noted for its luxuriance and
beauty, but see also the note on flowers and willows in the song
above. Chang-t'ai was a district of Ch'ang-an where lived a famous
T'ang courtesan named Liu, i.e., "willow"; *Chang-t'ai liu* is often
used in reference to courtesans generally.

c 我也會唱鷓鴣舞垂手
   (uô iê huəî) chiàng zhiē gū, vû chuəî shioû   ttp *tpt* r
   I know how to sing the Che-ku, dance the
      Ch'ui-shou,[32]

d 會打圍會蹴踘
   huəî dâ uəî, huəî dziù.[33] giû.   ttp *ttt* r
   Drive game for the hunt, kick the football,

e 會圍棋會雙陸
   huəî uəî kî, huəî shuāng lioù.   t*pp* *tpt* r
   play chess and roll dice;

f 你便是落了我牙歪了我口
   (nî bièn shî) luò. (liau) uô á, uaî (liau) uô koû   ttp *ptt* r
   Even if you knock out my teeth, stretch my
      mouth out of shape,

g 瘸了我腿折了我手
   kiué (liau) uô tuəî, zhiê. (liau) uô shioû   p*tt* *ttt* r
   Lame my legs, break my arms,

h 天與我這幾般兒歹症候
   (tiēn iû uô zhiê gî bàn r̂) daî zhiə̀ng hoù   *ttt* r
   Even if heaven afflicted me with these several
      ills and disabilities,

   尚兀自不肯休
   (shiàng û. dzə̀) bû. kə̂n hioū   ttp r
   I'd still not give up;[34]

---

32. *Che-ku* or *Che-ku t'ien* 鷓鴣天 is the name of a tz'u verse
form; *Ch'ui-shou* is the name of a song to which one danced, hands
hanging down the while.

33. *dziù* does not appear in CYYY.

34. In the *Pei tz'u kuang cheng p'u*, cf. Nan lü, pp. 15b and 16a–
b, Li Yü quotes this song as two shorter songs, dividing them at this
point, i.e., the end of sentence 4. The first part he calls a Shou wei
收尾, the second a Wei sheng 尾聲. In both cases, however, his texts
differ widely from other versions. He changed the final line of the
poem to fit the Wei sheng metrical pattern ttppcps, whereas the usual
Huang chung wei, being ttpppcs, is much nearer the last line of the
text quoted above. In view of this I prefer to take the song as a
Huang chung wei expanded in the manner of, for example, a hundred-
word Che kuei ling. This is further justified in that the basic structure of all the lines in sentences 3 and 4 of this version of the poem
is trisyllabic like that in lines 3 and 4 of the standard Huang chung
wei. Wu Hsiao-ling, pp. 949–53, divides the song on the basis of
Li Yü's analysis but calls the first part Huang chung wei, as the song

5a　除是閻王親令喚
(chiú shr̀) iém iuáng tsiēn liàng huòn   *pp* ptt
Not unless Yama himself gives the order

神鬼自來勾
shién guəî dzž lái goū   *tt* tpp　r
And the evil spirits themselves come to hook out

b　三魂歸地府
sām huə́n guəî dî fû   *pp* ptt
My three souls and return them to hell,

七魄喪冥幽
tsî. paî. sàng miə́ng ioū   *tt* tpp　r
My seven shades and consign them to oblivion,[35]

6　那其間纏
(nà kí gān tsaî)
Only then

不向煙花路兒上走
bû. hiàng iēn huā lù (ŕ) shiàng dzoû   *ttpp* pcs　r
will I retire from the path of mist and flowers.[36]

Except for sentences 3, 4, and 5 in the Huang chung wei, the metrical patterns at the right are based on Wang Li's description of the two songs.[37] As we can see, Kuan Han-ch'ing's Yi chih hua is regular but the Huang chung wei is about four times as long as it would ordinarily be. Wang Li gives the verse form as follows:

1. *pptt*ppt　r
2. *ttp*pttp　r
3. ttp,ttp　r
4. ttp,ttp　r
5. tpp,ttpp　r
6. *ttp*ppcs　r

---

form is called in the *Yung-hsi yüeh-fu* version, which he uses. By so dividing this version he ignores the fact that his last lines fit the metrical patterns of neither the Huang chung wei nor the Wei sheng. For this reason alone, to say nothing of the fact that the lines readily fall into the Huang chung wei verse form, it would seem that such a division is questionable.

35. The belief being that one dies only after the evil spirits have hooked out of one's body all ten of its souls.

36. "mist and flowers,"—i.e., the gay life, life among the courtesans.

37. HYSLH, pp. 808–9; however, he follows the *Pei tz'u kuang cheng p'u* very closely.

In his note on the Huang chung wei, Li Yü points out that the number of lines and words in this song is not fixed. He also says that
the final line must be tppcs, though there are no cases of its being
less than seven syllables. He mentions that there can be a great
many trisyllabic phrases used one after another (as in lines 3 and 4)
and that sometimes four syllables may be added after a trisyllabic
phrase (as in line 5).[38]

If we examine the groups of syllables Kuan Han-ch'ing added to
the first two lines of this song we can see that in meter they bear
little similarity to the regular lines; they are added as elements ex-
traneous to the line and build a rhythmic pattern of their own. In
lines 3, 4, and 5, however, whole line patterns similar to those in the
standard form are repeated over and over, or sometimes are matched
with a line in an inverse tone pattern. He uses many trisyllable
phrases to expand the third and fourth lines but they never keep
strictly to the pattern ttp as suggested by Wang Li. A syntax pattern
of 3-4, similar to line 5 in the standard form, is often used by writers
to conclude the series of trisyllabic phrases that make up lines 3 and
4; rarely, however, do they have such extended series as sentence 5
in Kuan Han-ch'ing's Huang chung wei.

Although san-ch'ü may appear to be free in form at times, or even
without form, we have seen that in all but the extreme cases consistent meter and verse forms can be traced. Inconsistencies that do
arise are easier for us to understand if we keep in mind that music
was the basis of san-ch'ü form. With but an elementary appreciation
of these matters it becomes possible to gain greater insight into the
Yüan writer's use of meter to express his themes.

---

38. See the *Pei tz'u kuang cheng p'u*, Nan lü, Huang chung wei,
p. 16b. In his pattern of the last line he follows Chou Te-ch'ing,
CYYY, ii, p. 49b. That the song is often expanded with many trisyllabic phrases is quickly seen to be true by a glance at the many examples of Huang chung wei in the *Yüan ch'ü hsüan*.

2
Rhyme

Rhyme, together with uniform metrical structure, was an essential part of ancient verse. Its origins point to incantation in which the same words or similar sounding words were repeated to achieve supernatural powers over the objects they represented. At this stage rhyme was probably used without conscious manipulation and was not always distinguished from assonance. But if at first rhyme words were repeated because of what they signified, later the reason for their use owed much to the pleasant sound they made at the ends of lines, and it was still later that they were striven after because convention demanded. In the fourth stanza of "Lu-o" 蓼莪 from the *Book of Odes* we can still hear the sound of incantation:

父兮生我
fu hsi sheng wo,
Oh father, you begat me,

母兮鞠我
mu hsi *kiwk* wo
Oh mother, you nourished me;

拊我畜我
fu wo *k'iwk* wo
You comforted me, you cherished me,

長我育我
chang wo *ndiwk* wo
You brought me up, you reared me,

顧我復我
ku wo *biwk* wo
You looked after me, constantly attended me,

出入腹我

ch'u ju *piwk* wo
Abroad and at home you carried me in your
  bosom;

欲報之德

yü pao chih *tek*
I wish to requite you by goodness,

昊天罔極

hao t'ien wang *giek*
But great Heaven goes to excess.[1]

Although this is a sophisticated poem in comparison to primitive
magic spells, it has the impact of a spell, reechoing, both through
sound and meaning, the key terms "to succor," "to nourish"; and
when the thought no longer focuses on these, the rhyme shifts.

The basic techniques of rhyme change little over the ages. It is
phonological change in the language that makes the most noticeable
differences in rhyming from one age to the next. Words that once
rhymed no longer sound alike and at best give to verse an archaic
flavor which can be appreciated only by readers with literary accom-
plishment.

Popular songs are done "by ear" in the sounds of the language as
it is spoken. During the Southern Sung, North and South China were
separate, and language in these two areas changed in different ways.
When the songs of the North spread to the South with the conquering
Mongols, they sounded unusual and presented difficulties for versifiers who wanted to imitate them. It was as an aid to those wishing
to write song verse in the northern style that Chou Te-ch'ing compiled the *Chung-yüan yin-yün.*

In comparison to the standard rhymes of tz'u, the rhyme groups set
down in the *Chung-yüan yin-yün* divide some vowels into narrower
classes. Groups 3 (-r, -z) and 4(-i, -əi) are not kept distinct in tz'u
rhyme books, nor are groups 13 (-a) and 14 (-e), groups 8 (-an, on),
9 (-uon), and 10 (-ien), or groups 18 (-am, -om) and 19 (-iem).[2] The

---

1. *Shih chi chüan*, Hsiao ya, xii, p. 22a. The rhymes are from Lu
Chih-wei, *Shih yün p'u*, p. 82. The translation is Karlgren's, from
The Book of Odes, p. 153.

2. Wang Li, in HYSLH, p. 732, remarks that tz'u writers were very
casual in their rhyming, and that this, rather than actual change in
phonology, was the reason for the differences in the rhyme categories.
He allows that distinctions in ch'ü rhyme groups 3 and 4, 13 and 14,
and 8 and 9 probably do reflect some phonological change from Sung
to Yüan but says the groups 8 and 18, and 10 and 19 are distinct in
Yüan ch'ü simply because ch'ü writers "were seeking to divide the

divisions most likely indicate some kind of phonological change, or, more accurately, the notice of it, and although they reflect the distinctions usually maintained in ch'ü, it is difficult to describe differences between so-called tz'u and ch'ü rhymes simply on the evidence of the rhyme books alone.

Certain rhyme groups tend to be used more often than others. The reason for this has as much to do with the meaning of the words in the group as with the total number of words in the group or with the sound of the rhyme. As a point of reference, however, the rhyme groups are listed below in order of highest total words (HYSLH, p. 732); those with similar totals are grouped into four classes:

	I			12.	-0
4.	-i, -əi			14.	-e
5.	-u, -iu			1.	-ung
11.	-au, -ao				
					III
	II			8.	-an, -on
7.	-ən			18.	-am, -om
16.	-ou			3.	-r, -z
2.	-ang				
15.	-əng				IV
10.	-ien, -iuen			9.	-uon
6.	-ai, -oi			17.	-əm
13.	-a			19.	-iem

A count of the untitled anonymous hsiao-ling from the ten ch'ü-p'ai with the greatest number of anonymous verses yields the following order of preference; those on the same line occur with equal frequency:

Over 10 percent
    4.   -i, -əi
Over 5 percent
    13.   -a
    14.   -e
    16.   -ou
    8.   -an, -on;   11.   -au, -ao;   12.   -o
    2.   -ang
    5.   -u, -iu;   6.   -ai, -oi

---

rhymes more narrowly," which hardly seems reasonable. In this statement we can see again problems arising from artificial generic divisions that do not take sufficiently into account geographical isolation, relative time of development, and nature of the verse transmitted. Compounding the possible error is the fact that he relies for his conclusions on the rhyme books, which are no certain reflection of practice.

Five percent or less
15. -əng
3. -r, -z; 10. -ien, -iuen
7. -ən
1. -ung
17. -əm; 19. -iēm
9. -uon
18. -am, -om

For literary studies a frequency count of rhymes would be more useful if it could be related to the comparison of literary and colloquial styles. Assuming that colloquial style is in higher proportion in untitled anonymous verse, we can compare the list above with a similar list made by Wang Li (HYSLH, p. 733) from the verses in the *Pei tz'u kuang cheng p'u*. If we assume the higher proportion of the verses he counted to be in literary style we can get an impression of rhyme sounds favored in either style:[3]

Over 10 percent
4. -i, -əi
16. -ou
Over 5 percent
5. -u, -iu; 11. -au, -ao; 10. -ien, -iuen
13. -a; 6. -ai, -oi
15. -əng; 2. -ang
Five percent or less
12. -o; 7. -ən; 8. -an, -on; 1. -ung
3. -r, -z; 14. -e; 18. -am, -om
19. -iem; 17. -əm; 9. -uon

That rhyme group 4 occupies first position in either list is owing to its greater total of words. Group 16 is high in both lists, undoubtedly because of its many popular words among which are *tsioŭ* "autumn," *lioŭ* "to flow," *lioŭ* "to keep," *loŭ* "house," *choŭ* "sorrow." The greatest contrast between the two lists is in groups 14, 10, 8, 6, and 5, groups 8 and 14 being preferred in the untitled anonymous verses, and groups 5, 6, and 10 in the verses from the *Pei tz'u kuang cheng p'u*. The list of untitled anonymous verses deviates much more than Wang Li's from the list that is arranged according to the highest total words per group. This may be owing to the tendency of writers with literary training to attempt difficult rhymes as a tour de force. Folk writers are less prone to this; their use of rhyme words is more likely to be prompted by ease of choice or theme of the song.

---

3. The assumptions in these statements are not without grounds as the *Pei tz'u kuang cheng p'u* favors "good" verse by traditional standards. However, as both my count and Wang Li's were made from a limited number of verses, the results are hardly conclusive.

Coming rather late in the history of Chinese literature, san-ch'ü shows complexities in its techniques of rhyming that reflect both literary influence and linguistic change. General practice bears out the following points usually held to be typical of ch'ü:

1. Syllables of different tones are rhymed, even those that were formerly in the entering tones (see Introduction). Compare *lü-shih* 律詩, in which only p'ing tone rhymes are allowed, and old style shih and tz'u, in which rhyming in other tones is allowed but all rhymes are to be in the same tone class.
2. Rhyme schemes are kept to one rhyme throughout. In t'ao-shu this serves to bind the songs into a unit more effectively than if each song had whatever rhyme was convenient for the writer. Unlike tz'u registers, ch'ü registers give no instances of san-ch'ü with varied rhyme schemes, but this does not give an accurate impression of rhyming in hsiao-ling. We shall shortly see examples using techniques that create the same effect as mixed rhyme schemes.
3. Although it is avoided in shih and tz'u, there was no objection to using the same word more than once in the rhyme scheme of san-ch'ü. Again this applies more generally to t'ao-shu in which a set of five songs could require as many as forty rhyme words. In hsiao-ling, duplicating a word is avoided by careful writers, though in colloquial verse it is not uncommon.

As for general techniques of rhyming in san-ch'ü, much can be learned from ch'ü registers which—at least the good ones—will show what is most "correct" and what is allowed. Owing to the prescriptive nature of these books there is no attempt to show extremes or even the usual limits of practice. Examination of a few verse forms reveals interesting variations from standard form, especially in colloquial verse. The verse form Shui hsien-tzu, for example, is composed of a triplet, a couplet, and another triplet; each line should rhyme except for the first line of the second triplet where rhyme is optional.[4] In most of the thirty anonymous verses in that form the optional line is rhymed; there are several instances of entering tone words rhyming with words in the other tones, as one would expect from the arrangement of tones in the *Chung-yüan yin-yün*. Two verses have "wrong" rhymes in crucial places, that is, the second line of the couplet and the last line of the verse, and there are a few cases in which final nasals are mixed, the most flagrant example being the following verse:

Anonymous: Shuang tiao, Shui hsien-tzu, no title. (YJHLC, p. 269; CYSC, p. 1756)

---

4. Luo K'ang-lieh, *Pei hsiao-ling wen-tzu p'u*, p. 99.

1a 火燒袄廟柱留情
   huô shiaū hiēn miaù iuāng lioú tsiéng   xpxttpp   r
   Fire burns Zarathustra's temple, no use to
     harbor love,

b 水淨藍橋空至誠
   shuəî àm lám kiaú kūng zhî chiéng   xtppxtp   r
   Flood covers the Blue Bridge, in vain to keep
     such trust.[5]

c 一箇魚沉一箇雁杳無音信
   (î. go) iú chiém (î. go) àn iaû vú iəm siən   xpxtppt   r
   A fish swims deep, a goose is far, there is no
     letter;[6]

2a 困書生憔悴損
   (kuən) shiū shēng tsiaú tsuəî suən   ppxcs   r
   Tired scholar, pining away,

b 想起來苦痛傷心
   siâng (kî) laî kû tùng shiāng siəm   ppxtpp   r
   To think of it is painful heartbreak.

3a 支楞的瑤琴上絃斷
   (zhī léng di. iaú) kiém (shiàng) hién duòn   ppt
   Tung, the string snaps on the jade lute;

b 吉丁的搯折玉簪
   (gî. diāng di. diēm[7]) zhié. iù. zhəm   xts   r
   Click, the jade hairpin snaps;

c 撲通的井墜銀瓶
   (pû. tūng di.) dziāng zhuəî iən piéng   xtpp   r
   With a clatter, the silver flask falls down the
     well.

---

5. These two allusions usually occur in parallel. The first probably refers to the story of a princess of Northern Ch'i who accidentally came across the son of her nurse sleeping in the Zarathustrian temple. When he awoke she fled but he became so impassioned that the heat in his heart caused the temple to burn down. The second allusion refers to a certain Wei Sheng 尾生 of ancient times who made a tryst with his lady love at the river by the Blue Bridge. She did not come but he determined to wait; meanwhile a flood suddenly came, but rather than break the tryst he clung to a pillar of the bridge and was drowned.

6. The fish and goose are both believed to be messengers.

7. 搯—probably for 掐, meaning 捻, "to twist between the fingers."

Had the writer been consistent within the sentence divisions of the song one might think he was seeking variety in the rhyme scheme, but he was not consistent. It is worth noting that even though the endings differ, the rhyme words are all from groups 7, 15, or 17, where the vowel is the same, -ə, and the distinguishing feature is the ending, -n, -ng, -m. Assonances such as these are used now and again in san-ch'ü instead of rhyme but it is never possible to tell whether the writer made no distinction between endings like -n, -ng, or -m, or whether he was simply being casual in his rhyming.

The rhyme scheme of a verse form, though now usually accepted as fixed by tradition, at early stages in the creation of the song must have left the composer with considerable latitude. To be effective, rhymes should come at the natural breaks in the stanza, such as the ends of lines or sentence divisions, and in most san-ch'ü this is carried into practice. The tendency in songs like Hsi ch'un lai, Shui hsien-tzu, and Yüeh chin ching is to rhyme every line, and this is so even in colloquial verse. Che kuei ling, P'u t'ien lo, and Wu yeh-er, on the other hand, rhyme consistently at the natural breaks of the stanza, but between these breaks avoiding rhyme seems almost obligatory. The standard form of Che kuei ling, in number of words per line and lines per sentence, is:

6r, 4 4r, 4 4 4r, 7r 7r, 4r 4 4r

Besides the rhyme at the natural breaks, there is rhyme consistently only at the seventh and ninth lines. P'u t'ien lo is a similar example

3 3r, 4 4r, 3 3r, 7r 7r, 4 4 4r

in which the seventh is the only line consistently rhymed, rhyme occurring otherwise only at the natural breaks. The short lines within a sentence stand more easily without rhyme. One might justifiably wonder why short lines are not more often left unrhymed in verse forms like Tien ch'ien huan and Wu yeh-er, each with a triplet of 5 3 5, all three lines of which are nearly always rhymed. We are reminded, first, that it was the song tune that determined line length, and second, that the meter and tempo gave emphasis even to certain short lines, which made the writer feel that rhyme was necessary in some places but not in others.

The rhyme scheme affects movement within the stanza. Certain lines can be emphasized with rhyme that makes the reader dwell, or feel he is dwelling, just a bit longer than either syntax or the stanza's pattern would allow on their own. In san-ch'ü this is well illustrated by the second and third sentences in the following poem:

Anonymous: Shang tiao, Wu yeh-er, no title. (YJHLC, p. 436; CYSC, p. 1723)

1a　長亭畔
chiáng tiǎng buòn   ppt *r*
By the side of the Ten-mile Station,

b　小酌間
siaû zhiaû. gān   xtp *r*
Between small cups

c　和泪唱陽關
huó luəî chiàng iáng guān   xttpp *r*
We weep and sing the "Yang-kuan";[8]

2a　人又去
riǎn ioù kiù   ppt
So now one must leave,

b　酒又闌
dzioû ioù lán   xtp *r*
And the wine is gone;

3a　跨雕鞍
kuà diaū ōn   tpp *r*
Mounted in the graven saddle

b　好教人千難萬難
haô gaù (riǎn) tsiēn nán vàn nán   xtppts *r*
What deep misgivings I have.

Because of the division between sentences 2 and 3 one expects
the rhyme at the end of line 2b. That line 3a is also rhymed makes it
seem as if it too were the end of a sentence. This makes the last
line sound like an afterthought, which can add poignancy, as it does
in the poem above, or surprise and humor.

Read as verse, san-ch'ü, like Sung tz'u, ring with rhyme sounds,
though sung to music the effect would be somewhat counterbalanced
by the melody. San-ch'ü writers availed themselves of the many op-
portunities to vary the effect of rhyme. In the following Che kuei
ling the rhyme sound comes from a meaningless particle used as a
noun suffix:

Anonymous: Shuang tiao, Che kuei ling, "Ch'iu p'ei, Seeking a Mate."
(YJHLC, p. 354; not included among the anonymous verses in CYSC)

1　春風窈窕娘兒
chiuān fūng iaû tiaû niáng ŕ   xpxtpp *r*
A beautiful maid in the spring wind,

---

8. Yang-kuan—another name for the "Wei ch'eng ch'ü 渭城曲,"
a song popular in the T'ang dynasty.

2a   嬝嬝婷婷
     niaû niaû tiə́ng tiə́ng   xtpp
     Lithe and graceful,

b   一捻腰兒
     î. niên iaū ŕ   xtpp   r
     A mere twist of waist,[9]

3a   百媚千嬌
     baî. məî tsiēn giaū   xtpp
     Countless charms,

b   得人心意
     dəî. riə́n siə̄m ì   xpxt   r
     What one dreams of,

c   可喜龐兒
     kô hî páng ŕ   xtpp   r
     A delightful face.

4a   俺也曾訴真誠的話兒
     ôm iê (tsə́ng) sù zhiə̄n chiə́ng (di.) huà ŕ   xtx, xpts   r
     I have poured out my heart to you.

b   扭回身休改變了心兒
     nioû huəî shiə̄n (hioū) goî biən (liau) siə̄m ŕ   xpp, xtpp   r
     When you turn your back, don't change your mind,

5a   哀憐我害相思
     (oī lién) oû hoî siāng sə̄z   xtpp   r
     Pity me in my sufferings of love,

b   鬧時節偷會工夫
     (naù shŕ dziə́.) toû huəî gūng fū   xtpp
     And from your gay life, steal a moment.

c   應副俺些兒
     iə̀ng fù (ôm) siə̄ ŕ   xtpp   r
     To comfort me a little.

All but two rhyme positions use the particle. This leads one to suspect that the writer was consciously striving for novelty. Usually such a device tends to be used to fill up rhyme positions and is useful because rhyme group 3, to which ŕ belongs, has less words to choose from than most others.[10] It is an easy way to get rhyme sounds

---

9. That is to say, a waist small enough to be encircled completely by the hands.

10. There are twelve Wu yeh-er, on the twelve months of the year, that show a more typical use of ŕ in rhyme positions. See YJHLC, pp. 435–36.

into a verse, but though there are verses in which, occasionally, other particles are used in the same way, the device is not widely used.

That a rhyme scheme is confined to one rhyme does not prohibit the use of internal rhyme.[11] As a means of varying a rhyme scheme additional rhymes or new rhymes added before the caesurae are most effective; however, rhymes at other natural breaks in lines or with extrametrical syllables are also strong. The following verse is an example of a new rhyme used before the caesura. It is the last of three poems on leisure by Lu Chih, who writes in a rather less colloquial style than is found in the anonymous songs:

Lu Chih (1234—1300): Shuang tiao, Ch'en tsui tung feng, "Hsien chü, In Seclusion." (YJHLC, p. 184; CYSC, p. 113)

1a 學邵平坡前種瓜
    (hió.) shiaù piáng puō tsién zhùng guā   xtppts r
    Like Shao P'ing[12] I plant melons on the hillside,

 b 學粊明籬下栽花
    (hió.) iuēn miáng lí hà dzaī huā   xpxtpp r
    And flowers by the hedge like Yüan-ming[13]

2a 旋鑿開蔬茖池
    (siuèn dzuó. koī) hàm tâm chí   ttp
    I have just dug a pool for lotus

 b 高豎起茶藤架
    (gaō shiù kī) tú məí gà   ppt r
    And set up high the vine trellis,

 c 悶來時石鼎烹茶
    mə̀n laí shí shí. diə́ng pə̄ng chá   tpp, xppx r

---

11. A shift in rhyme in the key points of the rhyme scheme is not common but there are a few cases. See YJHLC, p. 178, the ninth verse.

12. Shao P'ing was given the fief of Tung-ling during the Ch'in dynasty. When Ch'in fell, he was poverty stricken and for a living he turned to growing melons. These were so good that he became famous for them, more famous than he would have become in the service of Ch'in.

13. T'ao Yüan-ming—poet and recluse, 365—472, whose best known poem was on leaving office and returning to his simple but hard life as a recluse. See also the first of his twenty poems on the subject of drinking for his own reference to Shao P'ing in *T'ao yüan-ming chi*, iii, p. 10a.

And when my spirits are low, I boil tea in an
earthen pot;[14]

3a 無是無非快活煞

vú shỉ vú fəī kuaì huó shâ.   xtpptttp r

Above mean things, I am greatly content,

b 鎖住了心猿意馬

suô zhiù liaû siəm iuén ì mâ   xxx, ppcs r

The beasts of my emotions have all been
tethered.[15]

The internal rhymes in the first two lines make an effect similar to
lines with a rhyme scheme *abab*. This is pronounced because the
sound of *piǒng, miǒng* of the internal rhymes differs so much from that
of the end rhyme words, *guā, huā*. Compare rhyme in lü-shih, which
occurs predominantly in alternate lines and usually marks the end of
a complete thought, a distinctive use of rhyme rare in san-ch'ü. Un-
predictable rhyming permits a great variety of different effects, and
the sounds attract attention to the rhymed words which take on a
special emphasis. In the poem above, for example, this emphasis
falls on the names of two famous hermits, Shao P'ing and T'ao Yüan-
ming. By alluding to them and strengthening the allusion with internal rhymes, the author stresses from the outset the theme of the quiet
life away from the problems of the world.

Line 1c of the following poem carries rhyme at positions which,
though regularly spaced, do not have natural emphasis from the line's
rhythm. The result is a subtler assonance than that in the first two
lines of Lu Chih's poem:

Anonymous: Chung lü, Ying hsien k'o, "Shih-er yüeh, No. 6, The
Twelve Months, Sixth Month." (YJHLC, p. 49; CYSC, p. 1683)

1a 庭院雅

tiǒng iuèn â   xts r

The sequestered garden

---

14. *shí. diǒng*—"earthen pot" makes more sense·in English than
"stone tripod" and gives the correct impression of rough, simple com-
forts.

15. Literally, "I have locked up the [lively] monkey of my heart
and the [wild] horse of my thoughts"; this is a Buddhist cliché referring to the difficulties of calming the mind for meditation. Note that
the melons, flowers, Shao P'ing, T'ao Yüan-ming, the lotus pool, trellis, and tea in a stone pot are all references to a life of retirement
from society.

b　鬧蜂僑
　　naù fūng á   tpp　r
　　Is disturbed by the flight of bees,[16]

c　開盡海榴無數花
　　koî dzìən hoî lioú vú shiù haū   xxtppcs　r
　　The pomegranate have bloomed in countless
　　　　blossoms.

2a　剖甘瓜
　　poû gōm guā   tpp　r
　　A sweet melon is opened.

b　點嫩茶
　　diêm nùən chá   tts　r
　　Tea made from new leaves;[17]

3a　屈指韶華
　　kiû.[18] zhî chiaú huá   xtpp　r
　　I reckon the years on my fingers . . .

b　又過了今年夏
　　ioù guò (liau) giə̄m nién hà   xtppc　r
　　This summer, too, has passed.

The sound of the rhyming syllables *koî* and *hoî* fills the rather long space between the end rhymes of lines 1b and 1c. The -oi rhyme is close enough in sound to the end rhyme to create a harmonious effect and yet it is not as obvious as an -a rhyme would have been.

Even if the internal rhyme is the same as the end rhyme, rhyming at different positions in a line will cause quite different effects. For example, in the following poem, line 2a has a most interesting sound which comes from rhyming the initial, or metrically weak, syllables of the rhythm units:

Ch'iao Chi (1280–1345): Shuang tiao, Tien ch'ien huan, no title.[19]
(YJHLC, p. 275; CYSC, p. 630)

---

16. *fūng á* suggests the specific times in the morning and evening when bees issue forth from and return to the hive.

17. *nùən chá* "soft tea leaves" —the leaves that were picked when they were tender and new. *diêm chá* is a particular method of making tea in which boiling water is poured into the cup causing the tea leaves to float on the top. In this line I follow CYSC.

18. Here I follow the reading in YJHLC, but see CYSC, p. 1683n.

19. This is one of several sequels, by Ch'iao Chi and other poets, to the two poems by Ah-li Hsi-ying on "The Haunt of Idle Clouds," his retreat. Compare this poem with the second of Ah-li Hsi-ying's as it appears in YJHLC, p. 272, and his first, p. 106, below.

1a 懶雲窩
　　lân iuán uō   tpp r
　　The Haunt of Idle Clouds:

 b 雲窩客至欲如何
　　iuán uō kaî. zhî iû. riú hó   xpxttpp r
　　What does one want, coming to a retreat in the
　　　clouds?

2a 懶雲窩裏和雲臥
　　lân iuán uō lî huó iuán uô   xpxtppt r
　　In the Haunt of Idle Clouds to lie among clouds,

 b 打會磨跎
　　dâ huəî muó tuó   xtpp r
　　And while away the time.

3a 想人生待怎麼
　　(siâng) rién shēng daî dzâm muō   xpxtp r
　　I wonder about the purpose of life;

 b 貴比我爭些大
　　(guəî bî uô) zhēng[20] siē duô   ppt r
　　The noble are not quite as noble as I,

 c 富比我爭些箇
　　(fû) bî uô zhēng siē gô   xtppt r
　　The rich not quite as rich as I,

4a 呵呵笑我
　　hō hō siaù uô   pptt
　　Ho ho they laugh at me,

 b 我笑呵呵
　　uô siaù hō hō   xtpp r
　　And I laugh, ha ha.

Even though the poem is filled with additional -o rhymes, such as
the internal rhymes in lines 3b—c and 4a—b, the attention is taken by
the three-syllable internal rhyme in line 2a.[21] It is highly euphonious

---

20. *zhəng* "discrepancy, lack." The same in line 3c. For this
meaning, see Chang Hsiang, *Shih tz'u ch'ü yü tz'u hui-shih*, pp. 238—
39.

21. There is a standard form of internal rhyme called "three rhymes
in six words." It is rare in san-ch'ü; most examples are found in
plays with a t'ao-shu in the Yüeh tiao mode which has two Ma lang-
er songs occurring in succession. The second Ma lang-er customarily
uses the "three rhymes in six words" device in its first line. See
especially Wang Shih-fu's use of it in the *Hsi hsiang chi*, bk. 1,

and stands as the culmination of the sound of the first four lines.
But compare line 2a in the following poem:

Wang Ting (fl. 1246): Hsien lü, Tsui chung t'ien, "Pieh ch'ing, Sorrow of Parting." (YJHLC, p. 35; CYSC, p. 41)

1a   瘦了重加瘦
        shoù liaû chúng gā shoù   xtppt r
        Pining away and still pining,

b   愁上更添愁
        choú shiàng gàng tiēm choú   xttpp r
        Sorrow added on sorrow;

2a   沈瘦潘愁何日休
        shiâm shoù puōn choú hó rì. hioū   xtpp, xtp r
        Pining and sorrow,[22] when will it end,

b   削減風流舊
        siaû. gâm fūng lioú gioù   xtppt r
        Now that past joys wane?

3a   一自巫蛾去後
        î. dzè vú ó kiù hoù   xtpptx r

---

act 3, the ninth song, which is most beautiful. Chou Te-ch'ing makes
special mention of it in the CYYY, ii, pp. 45b—46a, remarking that it
must coincide with the wu-t'ou. It is significant that its only occurrence in the Yüan anthologies of san-ch'ü is in a t'ao-shu by Chou
Te-ch'ing himself (see TPYF, vii, p. 7a). It will suffice to quote only
the single line in illustration:

     看的可知見疾
        (kòn dî.) kô zhī gièn dzî.   pptp r

The line always takes the form of three two-syllable rhythm units in
which the rhymes can only fall on the final syllable of each unit. It
is in this respect that "three rhymes in six words" differs from the
examples of three-syllable rhyme shown in Chiao Chi's poem and in
the following examples.

    22. *shiâm shoù* "Shen's pining" —getting as thin as Shen Yüeh
did during a long illness. See his biography in the *Liang Shu*, xiii.
puōn choú "P'an's sorrow" probably refers to P'an Yüeh's mourning
the loss of his wife. See his three poems called "Tao wang" in *Wen
hsüan*, xxiii, pp. 23b—27a. As the names Shen and P'an bring nothing
to the English translation they are omitted. From the allusions here
and in line 3a we know the song to be written from a man's point of
view.

Since Wu-o has gone,[23]

b 雲平楚岫

iuán piáng chû[24] sioù   xppt r

Clouds hover on the peaks of Ch'u,[25]

c 玉蕭聲斷南樓

(iù. siaū) shiāng duòn nám loú   xtpp r

And the jade flute has stopped playing in the
south chamber.

Pining and sorrow, both key words in the poem, establish the
rhyme and it is the -ou vowel sound that stands out most clearly
among the sounds of the first two lines. In line 2a the same words
reappear, this time as second and fourth syllables, both strong positions within the line. Compare, for example, how much less com-
manding the -o rhymes in line 1a of Ch'iao Chi's poem are because
the fourth syllable is not rhymed; but compare especially the euphony
of Ch'iao Chi's line 2a with the rather stark effect in line 2a of this
poem. The key sounds in Wang Tang's poem are placed only in the
strongest positions of lines 1a–b and 2a, so that they dominate the
lines. With perfectly natural results, Ch'iao Chi left the sounds in
his first three lines in hazy focus.

Extrametrical syllables make noticeable effect as internal rhyme
depending on how greatly involved they are in the syntax of the line.
In the third sentence of the following poem by Liu T'ing-hsin each of
the lines begins with a phrase of three extrametrical syllables, and,
as is sometimes true of songs in this verse form, the last syllable of
each phrase rhymes with the end rhyme and sets up a pattern with
the other extrametrical phrases:

Liu T'ing-hsin (fl. 1368): Cheng kung, Tsui t'ai-p'ing, "Yi chiu,
Reminiscences." (YJHLC, p. 23; CYSC, pp. 1424–25)

---

23. *vú ó*—Wu-o was the goddess who descended from Mt. Wu and
shared the couch of King Huai of Ch'u. This and "clouds over Ch'u
peaks" in line 3b are references to the "Kao t'ang fu" by Sung Yü.
See *Wen hsüan*, xix, pp. 1b–5a, from which the reference to carnal
love as "clouds and rain" comes.

24. Originally 是; here I follow the correction in Lu Ch'ien's annotated edition of the *Ch'ao-yeh hsin sheng t'ai-p'ing yüeh-fu*, v,
p. 38. See the note.

25. *iuán piáng* "the clouds are level"—that is, they stay over
the peaks and do not come down as they did when the goddess met
King Huai.

1a   泥金小簡
     ní giǝm siaû gân   xptx   r
     Letters flecked with gold,

   b   白玉連環
     baí. iù. lién huán   xtpp   r
     Linked rings of white jade,[26]

2a   牽情惹恨兩三番
     kiēn tsiáng riê hǝn liâng sām fān   xpxttpp   r
     Remind me and arouse my regrets over again,

   b   好光陰等閒
     (haô) guāng iǝm dǝng hán   xpts   r
     That the best time of my life grows drab.

3a   景闌珊繡簾風軟楊花散
     (iǝng[27] lán shān) sioù liém fūng riuên iáng huā sàn   xpxtppt   r
     The sun sets, wind is soft on the embroidered
        curtain, the down of the willow scatters;

   b   泪闌干綠窗雨灑梨花綻
     (luǝì lán gōn) liù. chuāng iû shaì lí huā zhàn   xpxtppt   r
     Tears fall, rain spatters the green silk window,[28]
        the pear blossom bursts;

   c   錦爛斑香閨春老杏花殘
     (giǝm lán bān) hiāng guǝī chiuǝn laû hiǝng
        huā tsán   xpxttpp   r
     The brocade is patterned; in the boudoir,
        spring grows old, the apricot withers;

4   奈薄情未還
     (naì) baú. tsiáng vǝì huán   ppcs   r
     Alas, the hardhearted has never returned.

The extrametrical phrases in lines 3a—c are a common occurrence
in this verse form, although they are less spontaneous than other
kinds of extrametrical phrases. The tones are conspicuously regular,
the pattern most often being tpp. They serve here to ornament the
lines, but because of the double -an (-on) rhyme in each of the phrases
the sound pattern is even more noticeable. As the phrases are merely
ornamental and do not function very definitely as an integral part of

---

   26. The letter and rings are the mementos of the past love.

   27. Although CYYY does not give *iǝng* for this character, it is perhaps the best reading in this context.

   28. It was the custom to replace the paper covering on windows
with thin green silk when the weather became warm.

the line, they have less the effect of closely knit internal rhymes. In, for instance, lines 3a and b of the following poem, the rhymes work in combination with two pairs of doubled syllables, and because the lines are shorter the echoing between the internal and the end rhymes is more rapid and gives the impression of greater tautness than there is in Liu T'ing-hsin's poem:

Sung Fang-hu (fl. 1317): Chung lü, Hung hsiu hsieh, "K'o k'uang, Traveller's Life." (YJHLC, p. 53; CYSC, p. 1300)

1a   雨瀟瀟一簾風勁
       iû siaū (siaū) î. liém fūng giàng   xtxpsc r
       Rain lashed by gusts of wind,[29]

b   昏慘慘半點燈明
       huān tsâm (tsâm) buòn diêm dōng miáng   xpxtpp r
       The gloom is lit by a small light.[30]

2   地爐無火撥殘星
       dì lú vú huô buô. tsán siāng   xtxptpp r
       The stove is cold, I stir the few embers.[31]

3a   薄設設衾剿鐵
       (baú. shiê. shiê.) kiām shiàng tiê.   ptt
       How thin is the quilt, (like) iron,

b   孤另另枕如冰
       (gū liàng liàng) zhiâm riú biāng   tpp r
       Lonely, my pillow is like ice.

4   我却是怎支吾今夜冷
       (uô kiò. shì dzâm) zhī ú giām iè liàng   xpxcs r
       How can I keep away the cold tonight?

That line 3a is not a part of the rhyme scheme and yet carries a striking rhyme pattern makes a most effective turning point from the restrained rhythms in the first three lines to the tenseness of the last three which are so heavily loaded with added syllables. The extra-metrical phrases in lines 3a and 3b become associated through sound, as well as meaning, with the image of cold in the words "iron," "ice," and heighten the hyperbole of these lines. It is this association of

---

29. Lit., a curtain of wind's force.
30. Lit., a half dot of lamp light.
31. *dì lú* is a stove set in a small pit in the floor, similar to the Japanese *kotatsu*; after one puts one's feet into the pit a quilted cover is thrown over to keep in the warmth. *tsán siāng* are remaining embers.

sounds and the tenseness of the doubled syllables that function most strongly in sentence 3.[32]

Throughout this poem internal rhyme and assonance draw parts of the poem together tightly. Lines 1a—b have parallel sounds in the last three syllables, *liém fūng giàng* and *diêm diǒng miǒng*. In sentence 2, *lú* rhymes with *vú* and *huô* rhymes with *buô*, each rhymed pair spanning the boundary of two successive rhythm units. In addition to the rhymed extrametrical syllables in lines 3a—b, *kiǒm* and *zhiǒm* at the head of the metrical line both rhyme with *giǒm*, the first syllable after the caesura in sentence 4. All these sounds, echoing and reechoing, develop an overall tautness that is not easy to achieve.

A preoccupation with internal rhyme, such as Sung Fang-hu shows in his poem, might become objectionable in poetry whose lines are all of equal length. Yet san-ch'ü accommodates such sound patterns without difficulty because there is greater flexibility in the line, which varies not only in length but provides, as we have seen, much variety in the arrangement of rhythm units.

Feminine rhyme is one of the most frequently used rhyme techniques in san-ch'ü. Most often it is disyllabic, but occasionally trisyllabic feminine rhyme occurs. Most of the time it is used in the same manner as ordinary rhyme, but sometimes the writer seems to be striving for a special effect. This is probably true of the following poem which is an interesting example of feminine rhyme. The subject is the mole on a pretty girl's face which the writer charmingly explains by alluding to the popular story of Yang Kuei-fei, the concubine of Emperor Ming-huang of T'ang, who was made to hold the ink stone for Li Po as he wrote a poem upon imperial request having just awakened from a drunken stupor:

Anonymous: Hsien lü, Tsui chung t'ien, no title.[33]

1a 疑是楊妃在
í shǐ iáng fǝī dzaǐ
It must be Kuei-fei before me!   xtppt r

b 怎脫馬嵬災
dzǝm tuô mâ uǝí dzaī
How did you escape your fate at Ma Wei?   xttpp r

2a 曾與明皇捧硯來
tsóng iû miáng huáng pûng ièn laí
There was the time you held the inkstone for
    Ming Huang—   xtppxtp r

---

32. How to simulate these effects in English is discussed towards the end of this chapter.

33. This version is from the CYYY, ii, p. 51a. See also YJHLC, p. 35, and CYSC, pp. 1237, 1238n.

b 　美臉風流殺

　　məî liêm fūng lioú shaî   xtppt r
　　Your beautiful face so bewitching—

3a 　巨奈揮毫李白

　　puô naî huəî haó lî baî.   xtpptx r
　　Then that hateful Li Po, with a flourish of the pen,

b 　覷着嬌態

　　tsiù zhió. giaū taî   xppt r
　　Eyeing your coquettish charm,

c 　酒松烟點破桃腮

　　(shaî siūng iēn) diêm può taú saî   xtpp r
　　Spattered some soot of pine[34]
　　　　And blemished with one small spot your
　　　　peachlike cheek.

The feminine rhyme in lines 1a–b sounds fresh and spontaneous because the proper names, being more difficult to manipulate than ordinary words, lend a sense of fortuity to the rhyme. The last three syllables in lines 3b–c rhyme, but as effective feminine rhyme only the last two syllables are significant. They add much to the euphony of sentence 3 as we can see by comparing the last three lines of another version of this poem:[35]

3a 　巨奈無情的李白

　　puô naî vú tsiéng (di.) lî baî.   xtpptx r
　　But hateful, heartless Li Po,

b 　醉拈班管

　　dzuəî niém bān guôn   xppt r
　　Drunk, he snatched up the pen,

c 　酒松烟點破桃腮

　　(shaî siūng iēn) diêm può taú saî   xtpp r
　　Spattered some soot of pine
　　　　And blemished with one small spot your
　　　　peachlike cheek.

---

34. A name for fine writing ink.
35. Written by Tu Tsun-li (fl. 1320). It survives in the TPYF, v, p. 12b and is titled "Chia jen lien shang hei chih 佳人臉上黑痣" ("To a Pretty Girl with a Mole on her Cheek"). The version quoted from the CYYY is probably a revision by Chou Te-ch'ing of Tu Tsun-li's poem. The Ming dynasty scholar Chiang Yi-k'uei in the *Yao shan t'ang ch'ü chi* attributes the poem to Pai P'u. He makes no distinction between the two versions but merely says, "Some think it is by Tu Tsun-li." See *Hsin ch'ü yüan* edition, 2,ix:6b.

Despite the fact that it presents the action more forcefully, re-
vealing Li Po's mischievous intentions only in the last line, the rhyme
fault in line 3b detracts too greatly and what is gained in dramatic
force is lost in consonance. The first version is probably a revision
attempting to make up for the rhyme fault, and even though the action
is not so strong, the feminine rhyme carries sentence 3 very successfully and is the more skillful of the two versions.

The spoken language shows a higher percentage of polysyllables
than the written language, which is based upon archaic style. As the
language of most san-ch'ü is closely related to the spoken language,
it is natural that more polysyllables appear, and that they occur in the
rhyme positions as well. Obviously when the single rhyme syllable
is a unit of meaning on its own, it functions more strongly in the line
and its effect as a rhyme will usually be sharper. If, however, the
syllable functions as a grammatical place holder, that is to say is
only part of a word, there can hardly develop the strong semantic associations between it and other rhymes in the poem; its sound, not
its meaning, will be the more important factor. In English, where polysyllables are common in the rhyme position, such a point is less significant, but in Chinese the monosyllable is foremost in the literary
style so that verse using many polysyllables has a distinct quality.
    In the following poem by Kuan Han-ch'ing there is such a poly-
syllabic word with final syllables that are grammatical particles in
the rhyme position at the end of line 3a:

Kuan Han-ch'ing: Shuang tiao, Ch'en tsui tung feng, no title. (YJHLC,
p. 182; CYSC, p. 163)

1a   咫尺的天南地北
        zhr̂ chî. (di.) tiēn nám dì bər̂.   xtppts   r
        (In but) an inch, is the distance between south
          of heaven and north of the earth,

b   霎時間月缺花飛
        (shâ.) shŕ gān iuê. kiuê. huā fər̂   xpxtpp   r
        (In) an instant, moons wane and flowers fall.[36]

2a   手執着餞行杯
        (shioû zhî. zhio.) dzièn hiə́ng bər̂   ttp   r
        With the farewell cup in my hands,

---

36. The hyperbole is intended to express the feelings of lovers
who, being apart even short distances and times, find their separation
unbearable.

b　眼閣着別離泪
　　(ân gô. zhio.) bié. lí luə̂î   ppt r
　　Tears of parting in my eyes,

c　剛道得聲保重將息
　　(gāng) daù də̂î. shiə̄ng baû zhùng dziāng sî.   tpp, xppx r
　　All I could say was "Take care . . ."

3a　痛煞煞教人捨不得
　　tùng shaî (shaî) gaù riə̂n shiê bû. də̂î.   xtpptttp r
　　The pain keeps me from letting you go;

b　好去者望千程萬里
　　haô kiù zhiê (vàng) tsién chiə́ng vàn lî   xxx, ppcs r
　　My farewell is the hope you may succeed.

The phrases at the ends of the lines are all so commonplace that
upon reading the first or second syllables the rest of the phrase immediately comes to mind. That each inevitably ends in rhyme makes
the line even more satisfying. *shiê bû. də̂î.* in line 3a is the best
example of this. Being a grammatical unit, it is unlike the other
phrases which are all separable into adjective-noun or verb-object
constructions. Though purely as a phonic device it has little that
differs from the rest of the phrases, stylistically it is rare in rhyme
positions and shows a use of the colloquial language in san-ch'ü
that goes beyond a mere choice of vocabulary or the use of phrases in
extrametrical positions.

In the following poem Ma Chih-yüan's technique is based on the
single syllable. Here the meaning of each rhyme word is as important
in developing the climax of the poem as its sound is:

Ma Chih-yüan (ca. 1260—ca. 1324): Shuang tiao, Luo mei feng, "Yen
ssu wan chung, Evening Bells in a Misty Temple." (YJHLC, p. 206;
CYSC, p. 246)

1a　寒煙細
　　hón iē̄n sî   ppt
　　Thin wintery smoke,

b　古寺清
　　gû sẑ tsiə̄ng   xts r
　　The old temple is tranquil,

c　近黃昏禮佛人靜
　　giàn huáng huə̄n lî fuó. riə́n dziə̀ng   tpx, tppc r
　　Near dusk all the worshippers have gone.

2a　順西風曉鐘三四聲
　　(shiuə̀n) sī fūng vân zhūng sām sẑ shiə̄ng   xptppcs r

On the west wind three or four times the evening
   bell sounds,

b　怎生敎老僧禪定

dzâm shāng gaù laû sāng chién diầng   tpx, tppc r
How can the old monk practice dhyana?

In addition to their prominence as individual units of meaning, the
rhyme words stand out as a special feature of the sound pattern in the
poem. Except for the last line, the rhyme words alone have the -əng
sound of rhyme group 17. Ma Chih-yüan has arranged the subject matter so that each rhyme becomes a key word in the narrative movement
of the poem. The first rhyme word, *tsiāng*, suggests visual tranquillity;
lines 1a and 1b both project visual images of calm. *dziàng* at the end
of sentence 1 is the first word to suggest sound, or the lack of it.
Line 2a is strong in this verse form, not so much because it begins
the second sentence, as because it is the poem's only seven-syllable
line with traditional rhythm, having three syllables following the caesura. In this line Ma Chih-yüan makes the only reference to sound in
the poem, with the rhyme word *shiầng* actively signifying the coming
forth of sound. At the strongest point of the strongest line, therefore,
he places the most significant element of the scene, the sounding of
the temple bell, and his carefully established silence he just as carefully breaks. The last line is usually anticlimactic in this verse form.
Here it has the wry ending characteristic of Ma Chih-yüan. Even
though it was his insight into the details of the scene that enabled
him to build and resolve a climax so skillfully, much of the effect is
owing to his technical ability, not the least part of which is an understanding of rhyme.

If rhyme is one of the most important aspects of san-ch'ü, it would
seem logical that translations should reflect the rhyme of the original.
In theory this is true; it does not mean, however, that an English version must rhyme in exactly the way that the original does. To insist
on this in practice one must usually ignore the aesthetic effect of
rhyme in modern English. To be sure, many stereotyped san-ch'ü deserve to be translated with rhymes in the Victorian tradition, but even
by such standards the effect would be strained in English if one tried
to reproduce the same number of end rhymes and the same rhyme
schemes that occur in Chinese. Obviously the answer is to reproduce
not the rhymes but the estimated effect of the rhymes.
   Let us look again at the Tao-tao ling verse form; the third of Teng
Yü-pin's tao ch'ing poems will serve as an example (the second and
fourth were given in Chapter 1). The most distinctive feature is the
recapitulation in the last line. Although this arises out of the natural
contrast between the parallel lines and refrain lines, the effect would

not be complete without the rhyme. It is this recapitulation that one should attempt to retain in translation:

Teng Yü-pin: Cheng kung, Tao-tao ling, "Tao ch'ing, No. 3, Taoist Song." (YJHLC, pp. 7–8; CYSC, pp. 303–4)

1a　天堂地獄由人造

　　tiēn táng dì iù. ioú riə́n dzaù   xpxtppc r
　　Heaven and hell are of man's making,

 b　古人不肯分明道

　　gŭ riə́n bû. kə̂n fə̄n miə́ng daù   xpxtppc r
　　The ancients were unwilling to state this clearly;

 c　到頭來善惡終須報

　　daù toú (laí) shiə̀n ò. zhūng siū baù   xpxtppc r
　　In the end good and evil must finally be
　　　　recompensed,

 d　只爭箇早到和遲到

　　zhr̂ zhə̄ng (go) dzaû daù huó chí daù   xpxtppc r
　　It is only a matter of whether it comes sooner
　　　　or later.[37]

2a　您省的也麽哥

　　niə̂m siə̂ng (di.) iê mā gō   xttpp
　　Do you understand this?

 b　您省的也麽哥

　　niə̂m siə̂ng (di.) iê mā gō   xttpp
　　Do you understand this?

3　休向輪回路上隨他鬧

　　(hioū hiàng) luə́n huəí lù shiàng suəí tuō naù   xpxtppc r
　　Don't fuss like everyone else on the road of
　　　　reincarnation.

　　Teng Yü-pin's choice of rhyme words is imaginative; the words are most naturally incorporated in the sense of each line and betray no need to rely on stereotyped phrases. Though it is possible to trans-late this poem effectively by emphasizing other of its features, for the sake of discussion I have rhymed the following version:

> Heaven and hell are of man's own making,
> On this the ancients equivocate;
> In the end good or evil wins its reward—
> It's a matter of getting it early or late.
> Do you understand this?

───────────

37. Either in this life or a later one.

> Do you see it at all?
> On the road of life, stop protesting your fate.

We can see that two rhymes in the first four lines are enough in English to make us look for a rhyme in the last line. To use such a rhyme scheme in the Chinese poem could noticeably detract from the clear effect of the form. Similarly the internal rhymes in lines 1b and 1d give the Chinese lines a strong ring but would be distracting in English. To approximate the effect in English, one might use assonance or alliteration to better advantage than rhymes. Generally speaking, however, serious Chinese verse is nearly always more successful in English without rhyme.

To do justice to lines 3a—b of Sung Fang-hu's poem (see p. 59), a translator should strive to achieve the rhyme change in 3a, the internal rhymes, the intensity of the doubled syllables as well as the imagery, all with devices that can create comparable effects in English. The following translation of Sung Fang-hu's poem is an attempt to show what is meant by comparable effects.

> 1a) Rain lashes in sheets of the wind's might,
> 2   The stove is cold, I stir the few embers.
> 1b) The gloom is lit by so small a light;
> 3a) The bed is hard as iron,
> b) My pillow cold as ice,
> 4   How will I ever stand the cold this night!

Note first that lines 1b and 2 of the original are reversed in the translation. This is simply because it became very difficult to rhyme line 2 in translation, and to be effective at all the rhyme had to occur in the third line of the stanza; as there is no difficulty with meaning, it seems acceptable. Lines 3a—b are not as successful. They convey the image of cold very well, and that there is no rhyme helps, with the brevity of the two lines, to reproduce the turning point that occurs in 3a of the original. The intensity of the doubled syllables and the internal rhymes, however, is only partly matched in English by the parallelism of the lines and the tight clichés "hard as iron" and "cold as ice." The last line succeeds both in reestablishing the end rhyme and in reproducing the roughness of meter of the original. Whether the general phonic tautness of the original is effectively reproduced is more difficult to say. Despite the onomatopoeia in "lashes" and "sheets" in line 1a, the predominance of low key *l* sounds in line 1b, and the strong association of sounds and meaning in "hard," "cold," and "cold" in lines 3a—b and 4, the translation does not seem to have the cohesion of the original.

The technique of rhyme in san-ch'ü can be described as a stage in the development of colloquial verse. Except for the differences that the phonetic change in the language brought, there is little that cannot be found in earlier bodies of verse. The difference between san-ch'ü and earlier verse is perhaps in the currency of certain techniques, especially internal rhyme and the use of polysyllables in rhyme positions.

3
Vowel and
Consonant Patterns

Organized vowel and consonant sounds in language can give impact
to a thought or concreteness to a description, or merely provide ornamentation for its own sake, but most commonly they create the lyrical
qualities we associate with poetic writing. Because a line of verse
is capable of a great variety of sound combinations, hackneyed expressions can be given new freshness. In the hands of a good versifier, sounds are arranged for the best aural effect, sometimes to the
detriment of meaning, but a good poet who controls the sounds of his
words can direct the development of ideas or subtly change mood. It
is not necessarily true that a poet must consciously manipulate words
to create predetermined patterns of sounds, but when a writer with a
command of verse is sensitive to the aural effects of words, it is most
natural that not only the meanings of his words but their sounds as
well should be tuned to the thoughts he wishes to express.

As one of the techniques for making language in verse more pleasant and effective, this ordering of sounds may be toward evenness
and balance so that the language is mellow and devoid of harshness,
it may be toward vigorous style in which balance is established and
overthrown, or it may tend toward the haphazard patterns of sound in
normal speech.

Most often, sound effects in verse are found to be loose with only
sporadic bursts of color which, either by conscious manipulation or
spontaneously, are created through the repetition of sounds in recog-
nizable patterns. Such patterns, if they have not become hackneyed,
are unusual and attract attention. If the repetition is protracted, tensions begin to build and climaxes are reached and resolved, reached
again, and so on. A writer in ordering sounds in verse has the choice
of using traditional forms or contriving arbitrary effects with free
forms. In much verse it is also possible to see spontaneous develop-

68

ment of sound effects done either in concentrations of like sounds or
by using contrasting sounds.

For purposes of discussing vowel and consonant color the same
division as that used earlier of syllables into an initial and final will
be useful. The final, as before, consists of medial, vowel, and ending,
and determines the rhyme class of the syllable.

Beginning with traditional devices, three can be named that have
long been recognized in Chinese criticism and have even longer been
in common use in verse. They are *shuang-sheng* 雙聲, or a pair of
syllables with the same initial. *tieh-yün* 疊韻, a pair of syllables with
the same final, and *tieh-tzu* 疊字, a compound word of two syllables
written with the same graph. We will discuss the first two, leaving
tieh-tzu to be discussed separately.

The terms shuang-sheng and tieh-yün, according to T'ang Yüeh,
probably came into use in the Six Dynasties (3rd to 7th centuries),
though the devices themselves are to be seen in the earliest literature.[1] They are best understood as a fixed form of assonance and
alliteration with the condition that by Yüan times many of such pairs
were becoming hackneyed.

Li Chih-yüan's use of both shuang-sheng and tieh-yün in the short
poem that follows is not unusual in verse written by skilled writers.
In all the existing samples of anonymous untitled verse written to the
forms Luo mei feng and Hsi ch'un lai, shuang-sheng is noticeably
more common than tieh-yün, and in no single verse do both occur as
is true of Li's poem:

Li Chih-yüan (fl. 1354): Shuang tiao, Luo mei feng, no title. YJHLC,
p. 218; CYSC, p. 1254)

1a	斜陽外	
	sié iáng uaì	ppt
	Beyond the setting sun	
b	春雨足	
	chiuə̄n iû dziû.	xts r
	Spring rain in plenty,	
c	風吹皺一池寒玉	
	fūng chūəi zhoù î. chǐ hón iù.	tpx, tppc r
	The wind blows ripples, the whole pond is cool jade;	
2a	畫樓中有人情正苦	
	(huà) loú zhūng ioû riə́n tsiə́ng zhiə̀ng kû	xptppcs r
	Someone in the painted chamber has just tasted love's bitterness,	

---

1. T'ang Yüeh, *Kuo ku hsin t'an*, i, p. 13.

b   杜鵑聲莫啼歸去

dù giuēn shiɜng muò. tí guɜī kiù   tpx, tppc r

And hopes the cuckoo will not cry, "Return."[2]

Strictly speaking, the pair of syllables must be a semantic or
grammatical combination before it can qualify either as shuang-sheng
or tieh-yün, and the syllables of tieh-yün, furthermore, should have
the same tone.

It is not the quantity of these devices but rather how well the
writer makes use of them that determines their value in verse. *iû
dziû*. in line 1b is a fresh combination and effective as tieh-yün. The
near shuang-sheng, *chuɜī zhoù* in line 1c, is effective ornamentation
for lines such as these depicting the usual setting sun, spring rain,
wind, and pond. The pair *guɜī kiù* in the last line is skillfully used
shuang-sheng, appearing as it does in the strong position of the poem.

Although in the strictest sense *î. chî* is not tieh-yün, it would be
difficult to argue that the effect of such a combination is not similar
to that of strict tieh-yün with the same tone, especially since rhymes
in ch'ü are made with syllables of differing tones. Neither *tsiɜng
zhiɜng* nor *tí guɜī* in lines 2a and 2b have the structural unity of *î.
chî*, as the second syllable of each pair is linked more closely to the
syllable that follows it. Again, it would be adhering too strictly to
rule to say that these combinations are not effective tieh-yün, especially since Li Chih-yüan repeats the pattern along with this rhyme
in both of the last two lines. In the light of this it is justifiable to
broaden the definition of tieh-yün in san ch'ü to include any pair that
rhymes so long as the syllables are not separated by caesura or run
on to the following line like *kû* and *dù* of lines 2a and 2b, for example.
Note that because the caesura in line 1c is after the third rather than
the fourth syllable, *î. chî* is not affected.

Tieh-tzu is one of the oldest rhetorical devices in Chinese; it has
been a universal part of both the literary and spoken languages and
is still alive in modern Chinese. These compounds seem to be arbitrary coinages. Some are merely the repetition of a single word, like
tsiɜng 清, whose meaning in the compound has heavier emphasis, but
many others—at least judging from the graphs with which they are
written—have little connection with what the single syllable means.
For example, *iɜng* 盈 means "full," but as tieh-tzu it can mean clear
as stream water, delicate as a beautiful woman, or stately as a war-
rior, depending upon context.

Words thus made are similar to those in the remark, "This boy
'gingles' down the road; that one 'gumbles.'" The immediate impression of two vastly different types of behavior is not suggested by any
meaning the words may have on their own but rather by a vague mean-

---

2. On the cuckoo, see note 8 in Chapter 5.

ing the sounds take in context. If, however, the first consonant of
gingles and gumbles is changed to "m," each word then draws to it a
definite semantic value independent of the present context and confuses the image that was created by the meaningless sounds.

When such coinages through usage become part of a particular
context, they are assigned definite meanings and are accepted as
proper items in the poet's lexicon. New terms constantly appear,
especially in the colloquial style. When san-ch'ü were being written
it became customary to attach tieh-tzu to another word, and the three
syllables were used as one term. It is undoubtedly to new coinages
in this form that Luo Chin-t'ang refers when he says that tieh-tzu are
one of the characteristic features of san-ch'ü and account as much
for its freshness of language as extrametrical syllables.[3] The following poem by an anonymous Yüan poet illustrates the manner in which
they were most commonly used. It is the second in a group of three
songs all using tieh-tzu in the same way:[4]

Anonymous: Hsien lü, Ch'üeh t'a chih, no title. (YJHLC, p. 32;
CYSC, p. 1676)

1a 聲瀝瀝巧鶯調
    (shimāng lì. lì.) kaû iāng tiaú   tpp r
    Sweetly the deft birds' voices blend,

b 舞翩翩粉蝶飄
    (vū piēn piēn) fān dié. piaū   tpp r
    Lightly the white moths flutter.

2a 忙劫劫蜂翅穿花
    (máng giê. giê.) fūng chř chiuēn huā   xtpp *r*
    Busily bees fly through the flowers,

b 鬧炒炒燕子尋巢
    (naù chaû chaû) ièn dzẑ siśm chaú   xtpp r
    Chattering, the swallows seek nests.

3a 喜孜孜尋芳鬥草
    hî dzẑ dzẑ siśm fāng doù tsaû   txx, pptt r
    Frolicking, (we) look for the sweetest herbs,[5]

---

3. CKSCS, pp. 31–32. Liang T'ing-nan in his *Ch'ü hua*, iv, pp.
9b–10b, has a list of the expressions that are typical of the style in
Yüan times. For general discussions of tieh-tzu see T'ang Yüeh, i,
pp. 81–90, and Ch'en Wang-tao, *Hsiu-tz'u hsüeh fa fan*, pp. 171–78.

4. The three songs are brought together only in the CYSC.

5. *siśm fāng doù tsaû*—a contest to see who could find the best
or prettiest flowers. This was a bucolic springtime amusement of the
young. It is possible that its mention here evoked the idyllic, but

b　笑吟吟南陌西郊

siaù iə́m iə́m nám maì. sī gaū   txx, ttpp　r

And there is laughter in lanes outside the town.

The tieh-tzu in lines 1a, 2b, and 3b all describe sounds: *lì. lì.*
describes the mellifluousness of the orioles singing, *chaû chaû* the
excited twittering of swallows, and *iə́m iə́m* the sound of voices. In
the same manner that these words describe sounds, the tieh-tzu in
lines 1b, 2a, and 3a describe actions or attitudes. *Piēn piēn*, long
established in literary style, has an accepted definition associated
with the lightness of a bird in flight. On their own, *giê. giê.* and *dzz̄*
dzz̄ both signify diligent, ceaseless activity. In line 2a this is fitting,
but in line 3a *dzz̄ dzz̄* expresses gaiety. Of all the tieh-tzu in this
poem this compound is most flexible; besides the meaning it expresses
here, it is, for example, used to show distress and unhappiness as in
kû dzz̄ dzz̄ 苦孜孜. But regardless of intrinsic meaning, these compounds, whose sounds add color and concreteness to the activity described in context, give a line brevity that would be impossible with
literal description. This is why they are difficult to translate well.

The following poem by Ch'iao Chi is a tour de force in which the
tieh-tzu make a pleasant ornamentation:

Ch'iao Chi: Yüeh tiao, T'ien ching sha, "Chi shih, No. 4, Occasional
Poems." (YJHLC, p. 394; CYSC, p. 592)

1a　鶯鶯燕燕春春

iāng iāng ièn ièn chiuə̄n chiuə̄n   xpxtpp　r

Everywhere orioles and swallows, everywhere spring,

b　花花柳柳真真

huā huā lioû lioû zhiə̄n zhiə̄n   xpxtpp　r

Flowers and willows burst forth everywhere,[6]

c　事事風風韻韻

shì shì fūng fūng iuə̀n iuə̀n   xtxptx　r

All things have grace and charm.

2a　嬌嬌嫩嫩

giaū giaū huə̀n huə̀n   xpxt　*r*

Beautiful and young,

b　停停當當人人

tiə̄ng tiə̄ng dàng dàng riə́n riə́n   xpxtpp　r

My perfectly graceful one.

---

the expression has come to mean also "looking for women," so the
innocence of the English line may not be entirely appropriate.
6. *zhiə̄n zhiə̄n* "to stand out clearly."

The tieh-tzu give the lines movement and lightness. They may be taken to convey things in profusion or they may be taken to function as diminutives and the soft tenderness in the talk of lovers. It is interesting to notice the subtle difference between tieh-tzu as concrete nouns and tieh-tzu as abstract qualities. In lines la and lb *iə̄ng iə̄ng ien ien, huā huā liou̯ liou̯* are like the enumeration of many separate things, whereas *giau̯ giau̯ nuə̀n nuə̀n, tiə̄ng tiə̄ng dàng dàng* intensify one single idea.

This device, used even in only two or three lines, is not found as often in hsiao-ling as it is in t'ao-shu[7] or the plays, in which it has a variety of applications. Most often one finds it in connection with themes of unhappiness and desperation, and a high intensity of emotion is achieved by it.[8]

Meaningless syllables of differing sounds were used occasionally in san-ch'ü, creating effects similar to tieh-tzu. In the spoken language during Yüan there were certain curious expressions, like the modern expression 黑咕隆冬的, meaning simply 黑 "black." Such are the syllables used by Chou Wen-chih to heighten the effect of his poem on autumn melancholy:

Chou Wen-chih (d. 1334): Cheng kung, Tao-tao ling, "Pei ch'iu, Autumn Sadness." (YJHLC, p. 9; CYSC, pp. 552—53)

la 叮叮噹噹鐵馬兒乞留玎琅鬧

diə̄ng (diə̄ng) dāng (dāng) tiê. mâ (r̀) kî. (liou̯)
    diə̄ng (láng) nau̯   xpxtppc r
Ting-tang, ting-tang, eave bells' rattling-
    brattling noise,

b 啾啾唧唧促織兒依柔依然叫

dziou̯ (dziou̯) dzî. (dzî.) tsiu̯. zhî. (r̀) ī (riou̯)
    ī (rién) giau̯   xpxtppc r
Kree-kirr, kree-kirr, crickets chirping-
    chirring cry,

c 滴滴點點細雨兒淅溜淅零哨

dî. (dî.) diêm (diêm) sì iu̯ (r̀) sî. (liou̯) sî.
    (liə̄ng) shau̯[9]   xpxtppc r
Dripping, dripping, fine rain falling-flowing murmurs,

---

7. A good example is Chao Ming-tao's Yüeh tiao, Tou an ch'un, "T'i ch'ing" (TPYF, vii, pp. 8b—9a). The first song is nearly completely tieh-tzu and the following songs burst forth with them in various lines.

8. The most famous poem using tieh-tzu is the t'zu *Sheng-sheng man* 聲聲慢 by the Sung poetess Li Ch'ing-chao. See *Ch'üan sung tz'u*, p. 932.

9. Becomes *sî. liə̄ng sî. liou̯* in CYSC, probably a misprint.

d　蕭蕭灑灑梧葉兒失流疎剌落

siaū (siaū) shaỉ (shaỉ) ú iê. (ŕ) shî. (lioú) shū
(là.) laù.　　　　　　　　　　　　　　　　xpxtppc r
Rustling, rustling, wu-t'ung leaves lisping-
　whispering fall;

2a　睡不著也麽哥

shuəỉ (bû.) zhiaú. iê mā gō　　　　　　　　　xxtpp
I'll never get to sleep!

b　睡不著也麽哥

shuəỉ (bû.) zhiaú. iê mā gō　　　　　　　　　xxtpp
Never get to sleep!

3　孤孤另另單枕上迷颩模登靠

gū (gū) liə̀ng (liə̀ng) dān zhiə̂m (shiàng) mí
(tsuō) mú (də̄ng)[10] kàð　　　　　　　　　xpxtppc r
All alone, lying on the solitary pillow in silence.

Typically, the first part of the poem is devoted to setting the
scene. Chou Wen-chih does this through sound images, and if we
consider the setting in sentences 2 and 3 we must conclude that
sound is the most natural viewpoint of the speaker of the poem. To
draw the physical features of the scene into the description of deso-
late feelings the person is suffering, Chou Wen-chih relies on the
agitation tieh-tzu can express. *diə̄ng diə̄ng dāng dāng* is not merely
the tinkling of a small bell but the persistent ringing that constantly
calls attention to itself; *gū gū liə̀ng liə̀ng* does not mean merely "to
be alone" but to be so lonely that one can think of nothing else, and
in this frame of mind all things, the wind, the rain, the chirping
cricket, and the leaves of the wu-t'ung tree, become contributing
elements to the state of melancholy.
　We need only to read the skeletal structure

> Wind bells rattle
> Cricket calls
> Fine rain murmurs
> Wu-t'ung leaves fall

to see how much the sound effects mean in the first four lines of the
poem. The onomatopoeic groups towards the end of each line carry
the sound images to a strong climax. Each is clearly resolved by the
verb in rhyme position which also ends the syntactic construction of
each line. This climax is built and resolved again and again until

---

　10. *mí tsuō mú də̄ng* "to sit motionless." This phrase is also
written 迷颩没騰. See Hsü Chia-jui, *Chin yüan hsi-ch'ü fang-yen
k'ao*, p. 28.

the last line, and its direct reference to loneliness justifies the ex-
aggerated sound images and resolves the whole poem.

Effective as the traditional devices may be, the spontaneous vowel
and consonant patterns account for the subtlest and best effects in
verse.[11] Consonants are like boundaries to syllables and may be
clearly defined, indistinct, or left out altogether. Vowels, according
as the oral cavity is restricted or open, i.e., high or low respectively,
regulate the amount of sound that is produced in normal speech. On
this basis it is possible to classify sounds in a manner useful to the
analysis of verse:

Consonants
    Class I
        a) p t k, b d g, ts ch, dz zh
        b) f s sh h
    Class II
        a) v, m n ng, l, r
        b) u iu i
Vowels
    Class III
        a) u iu i
        b) ə r z
    Class IV
        a) ai oi, ou, au ao
        b) e o a

Class Ia consonants produce the crispest sound in language; Ib
consonants are not so brisk nor do they allow the legato qualities of
the consonants in class II. The medials, -u-, -iu-, and -i-, when not
preceded by a consonant, act as class II consonants allowing the
voice to continue unbroken from one syllable to the next. Class III
vowels are high and do not have the sonority of class IV vowels which
are the most singable of all the sounds.

Classes I and IV therefore are capable of the most vigorous sounds,
class I for its staccato qualities, class IV for its loudness. The crisp-
ness of class I consonants can be dulled by mixing with medials and
nasal endings, just as class IV vowels can be made quieter with
voiced consonants which bring out the lyrical quality of the vowels.

---

11. Without massive research it is still very difficult to show how
the effects of spontaneous sound patterns arise, what connections
they must have, if any, to semantic values, what concentrations there
must be before an effect is considerable, and what relationship there
may be when differing personal, cultural, or literary viewpoints dominate pieces of writing.

The endings, -m, -n, and -ng in class II slightly reduce the sonority of class IV vowels. Diphthongs are classified according to the second vowel because a high vowel after a low, or a rounded after an unrounded, tends to close off the sound. On the other hand a syllable with a medial preceding a low vowel develops greater sonority as its sequence of phones is pronounced.

We can now examine a few poems to see what consonant and vowel counts reveal and what relationships to one another, and to meter, syntax, and meaning the sounds may have. We can begin by discussing a poem by Chang K'o-chiu on the reflections of a wife or lover longing for someone far away. It is a common theme and his treatment is typical:

Chang K'o-chiu (ca. 1280—ca. 1330): Shuang tiao, Shui hsien-tzu, "Ch'iu ssu, No. 1, Autumn Longing." (YJHLC, p. 251; CYSC, p. 761)

la   天邊白雁寫寒雲
      tiēn biēn baí. àn siê hán iuán   xpxttpp r
      At the sky's edge white geese line the cold clouds,

b   鏡裏青鸞廋玉人
      giàng lî tsiāng luón shoù iù. rián   xtppxtp r
      In the mirror the green phoenix makes a beautiful
            woman pine,[12]

c   秋風昨夜愁成陣
      tsioū fūng dzuó. iè choú chiáng zhiàn   xpxtppt r
      Last night's autumn wind brought sorrow in gusts.

2a   思君不見君
      sž giuān bû. giàn giuān   ppxcs r
      I long for you but cannot see you;

b   緩歌獨自開樽
      huòn gō dú. dzž koī dzuān   ppxtpp r
      Singing slowly, all alone open the wine:

3a   燈挑盡
      dēng tiaû dziàn   ppt *r*
      When the lamp burns down[13]

----

12. *tsiāng luón*—presumably the green phoenix carved on her hair clasp which she can see as she looks into the hand mirror. Because it is a lone phoenix, it reminds her of her own solitude and so makes her more melancholy.

13. This and the following line read literally, "(By the time) the lamp's (wick) is all turned (i.e., used) up, (from the) wine (I am) half intoxicated."

b　　酒半醺

　　dzioû buòn hiuə̄n   xts r
　　I've nearly drunk too much;

c　　如此黄昏

　　riú tsẑ huáng huə̄n   xtpp r
　　Such are my evenings.

A count of the initial consonants reveals a high number of voiceless initials in this poem, the proportion to voiced initials being
nearly five to one.[14] The exceptional line is 1b in which voiced and
voiceless nearly balance evenly. An examination of finals shows
that medials occur in over half the syllables as do -m, -n, or -ng
endings. The main vowels appear to be evenly balanced except in
line 2a which has mostly high vowels. Of all the parts of the syllables, the voiceless initials stand out most.

From this information alone one would expect the emotion in the
poem to be rather intense. However, there is no outburst of emotion;
loneliness is the point of focus in each line and the staccato initials
probably intensify it. If we examine the poem line by line we can see
how well the tensions build up with initial consonants. The first three
initials are all stops; the last four, by contrast, are legato and soften
the end of the line. The next line repeats the -n endings at the caesura and final syllable as well as the legato tendency towards the
end of the line; two syllables in the first half of the line stand out as
rhymes, as in line 1a, and the syntax matches the first line. In both
the lines it is before the caesura where the most noticeable sound
patterns lie. Line 1c has its strength in the last three syllables, each
with an initial affricate, the first two aspirated; the second and third
have the same medial and main vowel combination.

From line 2a to line 3b all the initial consonants are voiceless
and maintain a staccato texture that is slurred only by an occasional
aspirant. This is consistent until the very last line which relieves
the tension beautifully with its mellifluous shuang-sheng, each syllable of the compound having initial h- followed by medial -u-, and
each with a nasal ending.

By way of comparison there follow two poems chosen at random
from anonymous untitled Shui hsien-tzu. The first is on a lighthearted
theme: two lovers meeting and making love. Unlike many poems on
this theme, this poem ends happily:

---

14. Raw counts of this sort can afford only the most tentative conclusions. Before the number of voiceless initials in a poem, for example, can be considered significant in any absolute sense, it would
have to be compared to averages in prose and in other verse of the
period.

Anonymous: Shuang tiao, Shui hsien-tzu, no title. (YJHLC, p. 270; CYSC, p. 1757)

1a 後花園裏等才郎
    hoù huā iuén lî dông tsaí láng   xpxttpp r
    She waits for him in the back garden,

b   相抱相偎入綉房
    siāng baù siāng uəī riù. sioù fáng   xtppxtp r
    Arms round each other they go into the chamber,

c   笑吟吟先倒在牙牀上
    siaù (iə́m iə́m) siēn daû dzaì á chuáng shiàng   xpxtppt r
    And fall, softly laughing, on the ivoried bed.

2a 羞答答怎對當
    sioū dâ. (dâ.) dzə̂m duəi dāng[15]   ppxcs   r
    She grows shy, unable to speak.

b   不由人脫了衣裳
    (bû.) ioú riə́n tuô. liaû ī chiáng   ppxtpp   r
    Without thinking, they take off their clothes ...

3a 錦被裏翻了紅浪
    (giə̂m bəì lî) fān (liau) húng làng   ppt   *r*
    The brocade cover rolls like red waves,

b   玉腕上金釧響
    (iù. uàn shiàng) giə̄m chiuèn hiāng   xts   r
    And the gold bracelets sound on her smooth
       white arm;

c   恰便似戲水鴛鴦
    (kâ. bièn sə̀) hì shuəî iuēn iāng   xtpp   r
    It's like the drake and the duck playing in water.

A count of vowels and consonants reveals very little outstanding, all seem evenly balanced. The initial consonants stand about two voiceless to one voiced, as against five to one in Chang K'o-chiu's poem. Medials and endings occur in approximately half of all the syllables, and the proportion of high to low vowels is more nearly one to one than in Chang's poem, and they are more evenly distributed.

The first three lines show sound patterns strikingly similar to those in the earlier poem: lines 1a and 1b rhyme at the caesurae and ends of the lines. Line 1a begins with shuang-sheng, line 1b repeats the finals of the first and third syllables, and line 1c displays an obvious pattern in the last three syllables.

_____

15. *duəi dāng* "to answer." See Chu Chü-yi, *Yüan chü su-yü fang-yen li shih*, p. 277.

There are links in the anonymous poem from one sentence to
another: note the tieh-tzu at the head of lines 1c and 2a, the word *liau*
appearing third from the end in both lines 2b and 3a. As in Chang's
poem, the ending has special patterns. There is feminine rhyme in
the last two lines, and the last four syllables of line 3c have a special euphony arising from the similar sound of *hì* and *shuəî* and the
last two syllables' having shuang-sheng and nasal endings.

The second of the anonymous Shui hsien-tzu is a tao ch'ing poem,
quite typical in its treatment of the theme of escape:

Anonymous: Shuang tiao, Shui hsien-tzu, no title. (YJHLC, p. 266;
CYSC, p. 1753)

1a 　隨時達變變崢嶸

suəî shř dá. biən biən chŕng hŕng   xpxttpp r

I change with the times and so I change life's
　　rugged road,

b 　混俗和光有甚爭

huən siú. huó guāng[16] ioû shiəm zhŗng   xtppxtp r

I blend with what's common and dull the
　　brilliance, what is there to strive for?

c 　只不如胡盧蹄每日相逐趁

(zhř. bû. riú hú) lú tî[17] muəî rî. siāng zhiú chiən   xpxtppt r

Best to drift along each day in any old fashion,

2a 　到能夠喫肥羊飲巨觥

(daù nŕng goù chî.) fəî iáng iəm giù gāng   ppxcs r

And if I can eat good mutton and drink large flagons,

b 　得便宜是好好先生

(dəî.) pién ǐ (shř) haô haô siēn shŗng   ppxtpp r

The advantage I get is from a good former life;

3a 　若要似賈誼般般正

(riò. iaù sž gâ ì) bān bān zhiəng   ppt *r*

If you want, like Chia Yi, to be proper in all ways,

b 　如屈原件件醒

(riú kiû. iuén) giən giən siāng   xts r

And to be sober in all things like Ch'ü Yüan,[18]

---

16. *huó guāng*. This is from chapters 4 and 56 in *Lao-tzu tao-te
ching*, here referring to the poet's efforts to remain undistinguished
in life.

17. *hú lú tî* "muddle along." See Chang Hsiang, *Shih tz'u ch'ü yü-
tz'u hui-shih*, p. 504.

18. Chia Yi was a Han scholar devoted to the principles of Con-
fucianism. Ch'ü Yüan (B.C. 343–290), unable to convert his ruler to

c   到了難行
     daù liaû nán hiǎng[19]   xtpp   r
     You'll come onto difficult going.

In Chang's poem there were five voiceless to every voiced initial, and in the anonymous love poem it was two voiceless initials to one voiced; in this poem there are approximately three voiceless to one voiced. It is in the main vowels that the count is unusual; there are half again as many high as low against the more even balance of the other two poems. Medials and endings, as in the other poems, are found in nearly half the syllables.

Remarkable as the count of high and low vowels is, the distribution of vowels and consonants in each line lends itself to no noticeable patterning; the attention is drawn more to the tieh-tzu, extrametrical syllables, and colloquial phrases. Towards the end of the poem a rising proportion of voiced initials and low vowels makes a more sonorous conclusion, but this bears little relation to the burden of the last few lines. The most one can say is that the casual pattern-ing of sounds suggests natural speech.

The relationship between the sound patterns and the theme pro-duces special meanings in verse, and it matters less what theme and what sound patterns than that the manner of the relationship be seen to exist. The examples are sufficient to show that, rather than having fixed emotional values, vowel and consonant patterns take on their values from the other elements in the poem and the same sounds per-form different functions in various contexts.

Of the three poems, the first two have greater organization of ele-ments. The sounds build to a high point in the first sentence, and in the second they give unity. The last line closes with a conven-tional device that has a pleasant sound. All these patterns combine with the stanzaic structure to produce well-balanced verse. This formal balance seems to have little relationship to the subject matter or treatment of it. On the other hand the casual arrangement of sounds in the third poem does bear likening to the casual attitude toward life expressed in its treatment of the tao ch'ing theme and in a small way contributes to the mood of the poem.

In the previous chapter we saw how Ma Chih-yüan was able to control climaxes in a poem by choosing rhyme words skillfully. The same control is possible through contrasts of sound texture which can be used to signal a change in mood. Again a poem by Ma Chih-yüan illustrates this most clearly:

---

the "sober" or rational view in a world of drunkeness, drowned him-self.

19. *daù liaû* "finally, in the end." See Chang Hsiang, p. 382.

Ma Chih-yüan: Shuang tiao, Luo mei feng, no title. (YJHLC, p. 207; CYSC, p. 247)

1a   雲龍月

    iuán lúng iuè.   ppt *r*

    Clouds encircle the moon,

 b   風弄鐵

    fūng lùng tiê.   xts r

    Breezes toy with the eave bells;

 c   雨般兒助人凄切

    liáng bàn f zhù rián tsĩ tsiê.[20]   tpx, tppc r

    They make my sadness deeper.

2a   剔銀燈欲將心事寫

    (tî.) ián dōng iù. dziāng siōm shŗ siê   xptppcs r

    But when I trimmed the lamp to write down
      the thoughts of my heart,

 b   長吁氣一聲吹滅

    chiáng hiū kì î. shiōng chuaĩ miè.   tpx, tppc r

    My deep sighing blew it out.

There are noticeable sound patterns in the first two lines, like the alliteration and assonance of *iuán* and *iuè*., *fūng lùng*, and the feminine rhyme. The predominant consonant sounds are legato and are in harmony with the mood suggested by the visual image of the cloudy moon. *tiê*. "eave bells," the only consonantal stop in the first two lines, is the one word that suggests actual sounds the poet hears.

The legato sounds persist in line 1c up to the phrase *tsĩ tsiê*. which introduces the poet's sadness, the inspiration of the poem. The contrast between the sound of this phrase with its affricates and the rest of the first sentence punctuates the idea, "sad, deeply sad."

These first three lines with their lyric description of sadness abetted by the wind and clouds leads one to expect a new insight into the depths of melancholy. Instead the vowel sounds brighten, the consonants become more vigorous, and the poet is shown frustrating his own inspiration by overindulging in deep sighs. The surprise is basically from the meanings of the words, but it is made more effective through the contrast in sound which changes the mood projected in the last two lines.

---

20. In almost all of about 150 Luo mei feng collected in the YJHLC, pp. 205–19, the last syllable of this line has a ch'ü tone word. The only reading for 切 in the CYYY is *tsiê*. but it is possible that Ma Chih-yüan read it *tsiè*. as we do now.

Earlier it was mentioned that a skillful use of vowels and consonants could revivify hackneyed poetic phrases. This I believe
Kuan Han-ch'ing achieves in the last line of the following poem:

Kuan Han-ch'ing: Shuang tiao, Ta te ko, "Ssu chi, Ch'iu, The Four
Seasons, Autumn." (YJHLC, p. 271; CYSC, p. 166)

1a 風飄飄
    fūng piaū piaū   xxp r
    The wind blows swiftly,

 b 雨瀟瀟
    iû siaū siaū   tpp r
    The rain falls endlessly,

 c 便做陳摶睡不着
    (biə̀n dzù) chiə́n tuón shuəì bû. zhiaú.   xpxtp r
    Even if I were Ch'en T'uan[21] I couldn't sleep.

2a 懊憹傷懷抱
    aô naû shiāng huaí baù   xxppt r
    Distressed, I grieve over cherished hopes,

 b 撲簌簌淚點抛
    pû. sû. (sû.) luəì diêm paū   ppxtp r
    Dropping, dropping, my teardrops fall.

3a 秋蟬兒噪罷寒蛩兒叫
    tsioū chiə́n (ŕ) saù bà hón kiúng (ŕ) giaù   xpxtppt r
    When the autumn cicada stops singing the
        winter cricket begins;

 b 淅零零細雨打芭蕉
    (sî. liə́ng liə́ng) sì iû dâ[22] bā dziaū   xttpp r
    Steadily, fine rain beats on the banana leaves.

The phrase *sî. liə́ng liə́ng* in the last line usually refers to the
sound of wind but here it implies steadily falling rain. On banana
leaves the sound of rain is quite loud and the continuous sound becomes oppressive to one who, because of anxiety or melancholy, lies
awake in the night. A reference to rain on banana leaves in autumn
is standard in poems like this one. If a poet wishes to make his line
different he must do so through a particularly interesting arrangement
of sounds or through new associations with the old idea.
    Kuan Han-ch'ing's final line is most striking for its arrangement

---

21. Ch'en T'uan, a Sung dynasty Taoist who lived on Mt. Hua, is
alleged to have slept one hundred days without waking.
    22. YJHLC has 灑, I do not know on what authority.

of vowels, which fall into two distinct groups; the high vowels in the first part suggest the sound of rain both through imitative sound and literal meaning; and the low vowels in the last part of the line make a sudden contrast which imitates the sound of the rain as it spatters on the banana leaves. The success of the line owes much to this contrast between groups of vowel sounds. Comparing a similar line by Chao Ming-tao we find that the vowel sequence is nearly the same as Kuan Han-ch'ing's and that the initial consonants are as effective as the vowels in making the description vivid:[23]

淅零零細雨灑芭蕉

sî. liǎng liǎng sî (iû) shà bā dziaū

The tieh-tzu and repetition of the vowel *i* builds stronger tension than Kuan Han-ch'ing's line, but in the following by Shang Cheng-shu the climax of sounds found in either of the previous lines is broken by introducing an open vowel with *huó* and also by the nasal ending of *shiang*:[24]

淅零零和淚上芭蕉

sî. liǎng (liǎng) huó luəî shiàng bā dziaū

As the effect of the line derives from the conceit "tears mixing with the rain to fall on the banana leaves," the sounds need not be so concentrated as in the previous two examples. To these lines we might finally compare this line by Chang K'o-chiu:[25]

芭蕉雨聲秋夢裏

bā dziaū iû shiǎng tsioū mùng lî

There is no attempt to illustrate the meaning in this line with sound effects as in the other lines; Chang K'o-chiu, perhaps with a more sophisticated audience in mind, merely describes the banana tree and the sound of the rain in an autumn night. In all these examples the semantic ingredient is the same, yet because of their differing treatment of sound they each produce a different effect and serve different ends.

It is customary in traditional criticism to discuss a poet with regard to his diligent observance of meter, the polish of his language,

---

23. Yüeh tiao, Tou an ch'un, "T'i-ch'ing," the third song. (CYSC, p. 333)

24. Shuang tiao, Hsin shui ling, No title, the tenth song. (CYSC, p. 22)

25. Shuang tiao, Ch'ing chiang yin, "Ch'iu huai." (YJHLC, p. 363; CYSC, p. 791)

or the manner in which he uses allusions or figures of speech. It would seem most profitable to study a poet and his contemporaries by comparing their use of sound. A poet may be meticulous about the metrical structure of his poems and write in a most highly polished style but still be unimaginative in his use of sounds. Even with less than a complete study of several poets' works, the method used above suggests a useful approach to the critical appraisal of san-ch'ü poets. From the few examples in this and the previous chapter we can see that Ma Chih-yüan is one of the most imaginative.

4
Parallelism and Miscellaneous Repetition

Repetition is the most basic of all language patterning. We have already seen special types of repetition such as metrical patterns, rhymes, and vowel and consonant patterns. In those we were concerned with the arrangement of syllables of parts of syllables; here we will discuss patterns of repetition formed with phrases and lines of verse. As with the other kinds of repetition, repeated phrases and lines take conventional and arbitrary patterns both of which are important in san-ch'ü.

Of the conventional patterns, parallelism[1] is the most developed and in one or another of its forms dates from early written literature. Its point of highest development came in the T'ang dynasty, when its strictest rules were evolved. T'ang parallelism represents a standard and is a convenient measure of the parallelism used in san-ch'ü which is by no means as strict.

The two most important rules in strict parallelism are that the tones in each of the lines be inversely parallel, and that the same word not be used in both lines. This pair of lines by Chang K'o-chiu (YJHLC, p. 253; CYSC, p. 825) serves as an example, showing the inverse parallelism of p'ing and tse tone groups:

落紅小雨蒼苔徑
luò. húng siaû iû tsāng taí giàng   xpxtppt
Fall the petals in fine rain on the
    green moss path,

---

1. Many of the examples in this chapter are not in the strictest sense *tui-chang* 對仗 and so I prefer the more general term "parallelism."

飛絮東風細柳營
fəī siù dūng fūng sī lioû iə́ng   xtppttp
Floats the down in the east wind over
    the encampment of delicate willows . . .

There is also a special treatment of meaning in parallel lines such
that words standing parallel to one another are to be from related
semantic groups. This results in parallel syntax and sometimes gen-
erates semantic associations as interesting as those in figures of
speech. The semantic groups have come to be taken as distinct categories of terms dealing with, for example, the heavens or the elements,
with time, geographical features, and so on.[2] As it is difficult to
match every word exactly, writers often achieved the effect by carefully matching words with the most distinctive nature such as color
adjectives, numbers, points of the compass, proper names, or the like.
In the example by Chang, above, the semantic parallelism is quite
consistent: "falling petals/floating willow down" are as close as
one can get; "fine rain/east wind" might have been better if the adjectives could have been from categories more closely related; the
same can be said of "green moss path/delicate willow encampment."

The loosest forms of parallelism meant matching words according
to a grammatical classification, as nouns with nouns, verbs with
verbs, or grammatical particles with grammatical particles.

Wang Li has observed that the greater the tendency towards regu-
lating the metrical patterns of verse, the more a part of the style
parallelism becomes (HYSLH, p. 469). In the old style poems, parallelism is not so frequently used, and this applies to tz'u and ch'ü to
a certain extent as well. What Wang Li refers to is the fact that the
colloquial style of any age and in any verse form used a device like
parallelism with less consistency because of the sophistication required to manipulate it skillfully.

Chou Te-ch'ing has little to say on parallelism in general except
to remark: "[When pairs of lines occur], they must be made parallel;
this is a natural rule that everyone knows."[3] It is obvious that those
practiced in the writing of shih would interpret this "natural rule" in
quite another way from the dramatists, for example, and others less
inclined to write san-ch'ü in the literary style. The amount and kinds
of parallelism used in san-ch'ü, then, will depend upon the taste and
skill of the writer rather than on rules governing the verse forms.

There is a great disparity between practice and what the critics
held to be correct. Wang Chi-te echoes the remark of Chou Te-ch'ing
saying that it is careless if one does not use parallelism where one

---

2. For examples of these categories, see HYSLH, pp. 153—66.
3. CYYY, ii, p. 48a. The clause in the parentheses is according
to Jen Na's TTSFSC, p. 32b.

should, but to use it where it is not necessary is forcing matters.[4]
Again this is open to a considerable variety of interpretations, but
he goes on to say: "Parallel lines must be correct in every word and
cannot be acceptable unless they balance one another evenly. If the
first line is skillful, it is preferable that the second be skillful also.
It is 'one-sided withering' if one line is good and one not; [the bad
one] must be discarded and another sought. . . . "

He is speaking in terms of ideal verse, but just as with the other
traditional rhetorical devices, the applications of parallelism in san-
ch'ü enjoy a broad latitude. Two important points of difference from
strict parallelism are that lines need not have inversely matching
tone patterns to be considered parallel, and that it was not necessary to use parallelism consistently in certain lines of a particular
verse form. In other words, to achieve the effects of parallelism a
writer sometimes relied on syntax patterns and semantic groups more
than on tone patterns, and, depending upon his skill or whim, in the
same verse form he could choose to use parallelism or, on another
occasion, he could choose to avoid it.

A look at one or two verse forms will serve to show how much a
matter of taste the use of parallelism by san-ch'ü writers was. The
lines of the Hsi ch'un lai fall into the pattern

$$7 \ 7 \ 7 \quad 3 \ 5$$

in which the first two lines should always be parallel or, with the
third line, form a kind of three-line parallelism. Parallelism is most
frequently found in the first two lines; parallelism of all three lines,
or of second and third, does occur but very seldom. As one would expect, the percentage of anonymous untitled verse with the first two
lines parallel is lower, by about one quarter, than that in verse by
known authors, but neither approaches consistent parallelism.

In the Shui hsien-tzu, parallelism should occur at the beginning
and ending, as shown in the pattern

$$7 \ 7 \ 7 \quad 5 \ 6 \quad 3 \ 3 \ 4$$

with all three in either group parallel on occasion. The percentage of
anonymous verses with parallelism is only slightly lower than that of
verses by known authors. In either case parallel lines at the end are
preferred, but they occur in only a little more than half the examples.
At the most, parallel lines at the beginning occur in one-fifth of all
examples.

Even among writers with a literary background there were no fixed
standards. Chang K'o-chiu is the most consistent user of parallel
lines but Kuan Yün-shih, for example, whose skill is considerable,
takes a more arbitrary approach. Since parallelism is a sophisticated

---

4. Wang Chi-te, *Ch'ü lü*, ii, item 20, p. 126.

device with special ties to the literary tradition, it is one of the
factors most useful in judging whether a piece is nearer the colloquial or the literary style.

As a beginning it will be useful to examine a few poems that show
what can be achieved in parallel lines. The first two lines of the
following poems are typical of skillfully done conventional parallelism:

Hu Chih-yü (1227—1293): Chung lü, Hsi Ch'un lai, "Ch'un ch'ing,
No. 2, Thoughts of Love." (YJHLC, p. 92; CYSC, p. 68)

1a 閑花醞釀蜂兒蜜
    hán huā⁵ iuən niàng fūng ŕ mì   xpxtppt *r*
    Leisurely flowers brew honey for the bees,

 b 細雨調和燕子泥
    sì iû tiaú huó ièn dzẑ ní   xtppttp r
    Fine rain mixes mud for the swallows:

 c 綠窗香睡覺來遲
    liù. chuāng chiuən shuəĭ gaù laí chí   xpxttpp r
    From my spring sleep by the green window
        I rise late.⁶

2a 誰喚起
    shuəĭ huòn kĭ   xts   r
    Who rouses me?

 b 窗外曉鶯啼
    chuāng uaĭ hiaû iəng tí   xttpp   r
    Outside my window early the orioles sing.

The terms "honey" and "mud" are not, strictly speaking, in the
same semantic group but their rhyming is compensation, and because
they both occur frequently in contexts such as this, they are accepted
as a part of the same conventional expression no matter how dissimilar they may be out of context. It is not only the matching of words,
however, that makes parallelism effective; we can see from this example that much depends on the function of the terms in syntax patterns. Rather than through an intrinsic similarity of meanings, flowers
are related with rain through their both doing something in the same
way. Flowers brewing honey for the bees and rain mixing mud for the
swallows' nests are both contributing to the preparations for spring

---

5. *hán huā*, according to the version in CYYY, ii, p. 53b, makes
better sense; in line 2b, YJHLC has *liém* 簾. I follow TPYF, iv, p. 1b.

6. The CYYY version reads: "From my butterfly dream by the green
window I rise late." See note 28 in Chapter 2 re green windows.

and suggest in this poem, with conventional allusiveness, the stir-
rings of love.

Although in such lines two different sets of details are set forth,
they are such commonplace terms that the reader looks past them to
the images of spring and love which they conjure up. To impress the
reader with these images, however, one line would have been as effective as both together. That the idea spans two parallel lines,
charming as they may be, serves only to ornament the text; the two
lines together do not increase one's factual knowledge about, nor
make more vivid one's impressions of, the scene. The following poem,
which is in the same verse form, uses parallelism in a more functional manner in that each line contributes to the total idea expressed
by both the lines together:

Tseng Jui (fl. 1294): Chung lü, Hsi ch'un lai, no title. (YJHLC, p. 90;
CYSC, p. 492)

1a   溪邊倦客停蘭棹

     kī biēn giuèn kaî. tiéng lán zhaù   xpxtppt *r*

     Travel-weary I pause in my boat at the stream's
       side;

b   樓上何人品玉簫

     loú shiàng hó rién piên iù. siaū   xtppttp r

     Up in one of the houses someone is playing a flute;

c   哀聲幽怨滿江皋

     oī shiēng ioū iuèn muôn giāng gaō   xpxttpp r

     Deeply plaintive, the sad sound reechoes on the
       river bank;

2a 聲漸悄

     shiēng dzièm tsiaû   xt*s* r

     Slowly it dies,

b   遣我悶無聊

     kiên uô mèn vú liaú   xttpp r

     Leaving me sad and dejected.

Even though each of the lines adds much to the scene, there is
little interdependence between the two statements. One does not elu-
cidate the other nor is one line necessary for the interpretation of the
other; they are related only in that they are separate, though essential,
details of the scene. There is no question that one of the statements
is as effective as the two together, and again the parallel structure
adds only symmetry to the lines. If on the other hand two lines, through
parallelism, reveal significant aspects of the broader idea that they
express as a unit, then we can say that parallelism rises above orna-

mentation. Although his choice of details is not highly original, Wang
Po-ch'eng creates a feeling of loneliness in the first two lines of the
following poem that he could not have done without parallel structure:

Wang Po-ch'eng (fl. 1279): Chung lü, Hsi ch'un lai, "Pieh ch'ing,
Parting Sorrow." (YJHLC, p. 92; CYSC, p. 324)

1a   多情去後香留枕

      duō tsiáng kiù hoù hiāng lioú zhiə̄m   xpxtppt *r*

      After love has gone, the fragrance remains
         on the pillow,

 b   好夢回時冷透衾

      haô mùng huəí shí lə̄ng toù kiə̄m   xtppttp r

      When the dream is over, cold comes through the
         coverlet;

 c   悶愁山重海來深

      mə̀n choú shān zhùng hoî laí shiə̄m   xpxttpp r

      Desolation, sadness, heavy as mountains,
         deep as the sea.

2a   獨自寢

      dú. dzə̀ tsiə̄m   xts   r

      I go to bed alone,

 b   夜雨百年心

      iə̀ iû baî. nién siə̄m   xttpp r

      In the night rain, my thoughts go on forever.[7]

The statements in both lines are literal; no conceit draws attention
away from the literal detail to a figurative association. As for word
categories, all words but "fragrant" and "cold" match easily out of
context.

The emotional impact of the two lines arises from the contrast between the happiness that existed before the lovers parted and the
loneliness that exists now. "Love" has been experienced but it is
past and is like the dream one cannot recapture upon awakening.
"Fragrance" recalls this previous happiness but only in the light of
something left over. "Cold," on the other hand, implies not only the
present loneliness, but, being a definite contrast to its parallel term
"fragrance" and of what the fragrance reminds the person in the poem,
it emphasizes this difference between the present and the happiness
of the past. It is because of the parallel structure that the words can

---

7. *baî. nién* is reminiscent of commonplace salutations to a bride
and groom like "one hundred years' devoted love."

echo and reecho, creating more shades of meaning that describe the melancholy in this poem so poignantly.

Chou Te-ch'ing does not discuss regular forms of parallelism to any extent, but he does mention three special types with regard to san-ch'ü.[8] They are: *shan mien tui* 扇面對, in which the lines are parallel in alternation, for instance, line 1 with line 3, line 2 with line 4; *ch'ung tieh tui* 重疊對, in which the first line is parallel with the second and the fourth with the fifth, but at the same time the first, second, and third are all miraculously parallel with the fourth, fifth, and sixth respectively; *chiu wei tui* 救尾對, in which parallelism is used in the last three lines to brighten up the ending of a poem.

Chu Ch'üan of the Ming dynasty listed in his *T'ai-ho cheng yin p'u* seven types of parallelism that he considered important in san-ch'ü.[9] In their rather flowery names, they are: *ho pi tui* 合璧對, *ting tsu tui* 鼎足對, *lien pi tui* 連璧對, which are, respectively, two, three, and four lines parallel; *lien chu tui* 聯珠對, in which many lines are parallel with one another; *ko chü tui* 隔句對, or parallelism of alternating lines like *shan mien tui*; *lüan feng ho ming tui* 鸞鳳和鳴對, in which the beginning and end lines of a stanza are parallel; and finally *yen chu fei hua tui* 燕逐飛花對, in which three parallel lines make one sentence.

In addition to two-, three-, and four-line parallelism, and alternating parallelism, Wang Chi-te (ii, p. 126) lists as well *tieh tui*, which is the same as ch'ung tieh tui that Chou Te-ch'ing mentions. He also discusses parallel lines with end rhyme, and parallel stanzas in which the lines of one stanza are parallel with those of another.

There arises the question of how practical these definitions of types are. One is inclined to agree with Jen Na's comment on the ch'ung tieh tui of Chou Te-ch'ing in which he says that it is entirely factitious having little effect in the poem.[10] However, examples of a few are worth discussing.

Jan Na says that shan mien tui is seen rarely in shih and tz'u and that it was only in ch'ü that it flourished.[11] He adds that this alternating parallelism creates a distinct effect; this we can see in the following poem:

---

8. CYYY, ii, p. 48a. See also TTSFSC, pp. 32b–35a.

9. Chu Ch'üan, *T'ai-ho cheng yin p'u*, pp. 14–15.

10. TTSFSC, p. 33b. For some examples of ch'ung tieh tui, see Chou Te-ch'ing's own t'ao-shu, Yüeh tiao, Tou an ch'un, "Shuang lü." TPYF, vii, p. 6b; CYSC, pp. 1343–45.

11. TTSFSC, p. 32b. He includes the songs of the drama as well as san-ch'ü.

Kuan Han-ch'ing: Shuang tiao, Chu ma t'ing, no title. (CYSC, p. 1847, included under the anonymous songs).

1a 多緒多情
    duō siù duō tsiáng   xtpp *r*
    Many thoughts much yearning

b 病身軀憔悴損
    biə̀ng shiə̄n kiū tsiaú tsuə̀i suə̄n   txp, ptx[12] ·r
    Have weakened my body, haggard and thin,

2a 閑愁閑悶
    hán choú hán mə̀n   tpxt *r*
    In idle sadness, idle gloom,

b 將柳帶結同心
    dziə̄ng lioû daì giê. túng siə̄m   pxt, tpp r
    I tie the love knot on my willow belt.

3a 瘦巖巖寬褪了絳綃裙
    shoù ám (ám) kuōn tuə̀n (liau) giàng siaū kiuə́n   xptttpp r
    So gaunt, my red silken shirt is too large,

b 羞答答恐怕他鄰姬問
    sioù dā. (dā.)[13] kûng pà (tuō) liə́n gī və̀n   xpxtppt r
    Shy—afraid that she next door will ask about it.

4a 若道傷春
    (riò.) daù shiə̄ng chiuə̄n   ttx r
    If you say it's the dolor of spring,

b 今年更比年時甚
    giə̄m niə́n gə̀ng bī niə́n shf́ shiə̀m   xpxtppt r
    It's much worse this year than ever before.

    The metrical patterns of lines 1b and 2b, as in the strictest parallelism, balance inversely, and, as we can see, the tone patterns of Kuan Han-ch'ing's lines conform as well. But because lines 1a and 2a are the shorter of the four, and because their repetitive syntax structure is strikingly similar, they become the pivotal lines in the two pairs. Lines 1b and 2b have a syntax pattern of 3-3 rather than the more common 2-2-2 in the six-syllable line, and the unusual rhythm causes the lines to echo one another clearly. The last three

---

    12. This line and 2b have seven syllables in the four (and only) hsiao-ling collected in YJHLC and CYSC. See HYSLH, p. 813.
    13. In CYYY, *dā.* is a shang tone word but as the tones often change when words are used as tieh-tzu, and as the metrical pattern calls for a p'ing tone, I have used the modern reading.

syllables of line 2b do not have the same syntax pattern as those of
line 1b, but the similar rhythm which these lines have overrides this
difference. If the syntax of lines 1b and 2b is not blatantly dissimilar, the length of the lines, in contrast to lines 1a and 2a, would be
sufficient to create successful parallelism.

Although shan mien tui is more obvious if the alternating parallel
lines are of different lengths, there are verse forms in which all four
lines are the same length, and it would seem that unless the parallelism was especially obvious or the music repetitive, the effect would
have been lost. In any event, in san-ch'ü, and especially hsiao-ling,
these devices are somewhat of a rarity.

Chiu wei tui, used to make the ending of a poem stronger, is most
often found, when it occurs at all, in the songs Chai er ling and Hung
hsiu hsieh. The following song illustrates the technique:

Chang K'o-chiu: Chung lü, Hung hsiu hsieh, "Sui mu, No. 1, Year's
End." (YJHLC, p. 57; CYSC, p. 800)

1a 金蓮步蒼苔小徑
    (giəm) lién bù tsāng taí siaû giəng   xtxpsc r
    Her small feet[14] tread upon green moss in the
        narrow path,

 b 玉鈎垂翠竹閒亭
    (iù.) goū chuəí tsuəí zhiû. hǎn tiə́ng   xpxtpp r
    The crescent moon[15] hangs over green bamboo
        by the quiet pavilion,

2a 物換星移暗傷情
    vù. huòn siə̄ng í òm shiāng tsiə́ng   xtxptpp r
    Time works its change, secretly I lament.

3a 遊魚翻凍影
    (ioú iú) fān dùng iə̀ng   ptt r
    The swimming fish flicker the cool shadows,

 b 啼鳥犯[16]春聲
    (tí niaû) fàn chiuən shiə̄ng   tpp r
    The singing birds assault the sounds of spring,

4   落梅香暮景
    luò. məí hiāng mù giə̀ng   xpxcs r
    The fallen plum blossoms make the evening
        fragrant.

_____

14. *giəm lién* "gold lotus"—a euphemism for a woman's feet.
15. *iù. goū* "jade hook"—a poetic term for crescent moon.
16. See note 14 in Chapter 5.

As we can see from the metrical pattern on the right, lines 3a and 3b normally stand separate from the last line. When chiu wei tui is used, extrametrical syllables fill out lines 3a and 3b so that they are the same length as the last line, and the metrical pattern changes from the normal one, shown in A below, to one resembling B:

	A	B
3a)	ptt	xpptt
b)	tpp	xttpp
4	xppcs	xppcs

In recitation, lines 3a and 3b can be read as normal five-syllable lines, but they were hardly likely to have been sung that way. This is rather interesting because the lines, obviously differing in rhythmic structure, are effective enough as parallel lines to function as chiu wei tui, so one must conclude that the semantic element in parallelism is the important factor, at least in this song form.

By the way in which the normal stanza pattern builds toward the ending, a weak last line would stand out most awkwardly. With chiu wei tui, as the example shows very well, the last line is no longer a special point of attention, and even though it contains little that is different from lines 3a—b, it does not sound flat and the poem ends gracefully.

In the anonymous poem that follows we have an example of four-line parallelism, lien pi tui and lüan feng ho ming tui—first and last lines of a stanza parallel:

Anonymous: Cheng kung, Tao-tao ling, no title. (YJHLC, p. 9; CYSC, p. 1660)

1a　黄塵萬古長安路

　　huáng chiǝn vàn gû chiáng ōn lù　　　　　　　　xpxtppc r
　　The yellow dust forever stirs on the roads
　　　of Ch'ang-an,

b　折碑三尺邙山墓

　　zhiê. bǝī sām chî. máng shān mù　　　　　　　　xpxtppc r
　　Broken headstones stand among the three-foot
　　　mounds on Mang-shan.

c　西風一葉烏江渡

　　sī fūng î. iè. ū giāng dù　　　　　　　　　　　xpxtppc r
　　The west wind tosses a leaf on[17] Wu River
　　　crossing,

---

17. *î. iè.* is the classifier for "boat," referring here to the boat that could have ferried Hsiang Yü to safety. See the *Shih-chi*, iv, pp. 33b—34a.

d　夕陽十里邯鄲樹

sí. iáng shí. lî hón dān shiù　　　　　　　　xpxtppc r
The sun sets on the tree ten miles from Han-tan.[18]

2a　老了人也麼哥

laû (liaû) rién iê mā gō　　　　　　　　　　　xxtpp
How all this makes me old!

b　老了人也麼哥

laû (liaû) rién iê mā gō　　　　　　　　　　　xxtpp
How all this makes me old!

3　英雄盡是傷心處

iāng hiúng dzièn shr̀ shiāng siām chiù　　　　xpxtppc r
Sad places all for valiant men.

The words are skillfully matched in the first four lines, especially
considering the writer's added difficulty of maintaining not only the
ordinary rhyme, but of achieving two- and three-syllable feminine
rhyme. All four of these lines, and sentence 3 as well, have identical
tone patterns; in this respect the parallelism differs most widely from
that used in shih. Further, when composing four parallel lines, writers
of shih avoided using the same syntax pattern in both of the pairs
(HYSLH, p. 181); the syntax of the lines in this poem is the same
throughout. To one who is used to reading the carefully varied lines
of shih, these four lines may seem monotonous, but when the song
was performed with music as it was intended to be, the repetition, far
from being unpleasant, was very likely the song's strong feature, and
the other devices of repetition—similar content, identical syntax patterns, feminine rhyme, similar placing of the same vowels and consonants—must also have strengthened the song. We discussed earlier
the effect of the last line in this stanza (see pp. 64–65); set apart
from the rest of the poem by the refrain lines, it occupies the crown-
ing position. In the examples above, the last line, with its parallel
syntax and tones, has a strong formal link to the first four lines and
so its moralizing in abstract terms in no way weakens the ending.

The following poem illustrates two-, three-, and four-line parallelism, and in sentence 2 we have an example of what Chu Ch'üan
called yen chu fei hua tui, or three parallel lines in one sentence:

Hsü Tsai-ssu (fl. 1300): Shuang tiao, Che kuei ling, "Ch'un ch'ing,
Thoughts of Love." (YJHLC, p. 316; CYSC, p. 1051)

---

18. Probably a mixed reference to the T'ang stories "Chen-chung
chi" and "Nan-k'o chi" (or "Nan-k'o t'ai-shou chuan"). See Chapter
5, n. 6.

1   平生不會相思
    piéng shāng bû. huəì siāng sẑ   xpxtpp r
    All my life I knew not love,

2a   才會相思、
    tsaí huəì siāng sẑ   xtpp *r*
    Now that I know it,

b   便害相思、
    bièn hoì siāng sẑ   xtpp r
    I am tormented by it.

3a   身似浮雲
    shiə̄n sẑ fú iuə́n   xtpp
    Like floating clouds, my body,

b   心如飛絮
    siə̄m riú fəī siù   xpxt
    My heart, like fluttering willow-down,

c   氣若遊絲
    kì ruò. ioú sẑ   xtpp r
    My soul like wafted gossamer.

4a   空一縷餘香在此
    kūng î. liû iú hiāng dzaì tsẑ   xtx, xpts r
    Here, useless, a wisp of lingering fragrance;

b   盼千金遊子何之
    pàn tsiə̄n giə̄m ioú dzẑ hó zhī́   xpp, xtpp r
    Where is the longed-for noble wanderer?

5a   證候來時
    zhiə̀ng hoù laí shí́   xtpp r
    Lovesickness comes ...[19]

b   正是何時
    zhiə̀ng shì̀ hó shí́   xtpp *r*
    Just when does it come?

c   燈半昏時
    də̄ng buòn huə́n shí́   xtpp *r*
    When the lamp is half-dim.

d   月半明時
    iuə̀. buòn miə́ng shí́   xtpp r
    When the moon is half-dark.[20]

---

19. *zhiə̀ng hoù* "symptoms" generally refers to lovesickness, but
see also p. 40, line 4h.

20. Literally, "When the moon is half bright." *miə́ng* "bright" is
the adjective most commonly used to describe the moon, and as "half-

In poems of this verse form, lines 2b—c, 3a—c, and 4a—b are usually parallel. In the first sentence the parts of the lines that are
parallel all have the same tone pattern, the same word is repeated,
and the lines are not all of the same length. Although this is impossible in parallelism of the kind used in shih, we have already seen
that it is not unusual in san-ch'ü. Lines 3a, 3b, and 3c all express
the same idea but it is difficult to call them ornamental in the same
sense that we did the first two lines in Hu Chih-yü's poem. Being
repeated phrases with the same rhythm, they have an emotional effect
akin to that in the anonymous Tao-tao ling quoted just before. The
lines are shorter, however, and so the state of desperation they express in this poem has a special intensity that longer lines could not
have achieved. Lines 4a and 4b have the most effective semantic
parallelism of the parallel groups in the poem. In a manner similar
to that in the first two lines of Wang Po-ch'eng's poem, loneliness
is described in terms of contrasts, namely the contrasting situations
of the young woman and her distant lover. Through the two lines this
contrast is punctuated by the parallel words $k\bar{u}ng$ "emptiness," "lack
of hope," opposed to $p\grave{a}n$ "gaze after," "hope for," and $dza\grave{i}\ ts\hat{z}$ "here,"
opposed to $h\acute{o}\ zh\bar{r}$ "goes where." A good translation should somehow
show this contrast.

The theme of this poem is commonplace, even the ending has little
new in it. Its appeal lies in the sound of its language, as Jen Na
suggests in the statement: "In the beginning and the ending there
are several words that have the same rhyme [i.e., beyond the normal
rhyme scheme]; all are of the most natural sound. The last four lines
may each only be of four syllables but they are complex and each expresses the sentiment most clearly; this is indeed excellent writing!"[21]
The rhymes he refers to are the repeated words in the first sentence
and the rhymes at both the beginnings and endings of the last four
lines. These have "a most natural sound" because they express the
young woman's mood so precisely. The conclusion owes much to the
indirectness with which the images at the end are made. A lamp that
is half-dim is one that has nearly burnt itself out, the moon when it
is setting becomes dim partly because it is no longer directly over-
head and partly because of approaching dawn. That the lamp has not
been blown out and that the waning moon becomes noticeable means
one has remained awake late into the night brooding and unhappy

---

bright" it suggests waning light. Most adjectives meaning "dark" or
the like are not so natural with the word "moon" in Chinese and
therefore become either distracting or colorless. In the last two
lines of this poem "half-dim" makes a good parallel with a word of
opposite meaning, "half-bright," but in English this is not so because
a word suggesting light or brightness confuses the image; hence the
word "dark" in the English version.

21. Jen Na, *Ch'ü hsieh*, i, p. 5a.

with longing. The parallel groups keep the images in taut succession
and the poem makes a strong impression.

The final example with which we discuss parallel structure shows
that the rhetorical advantages of parallelism are achieved quite successfully even through the use of grammatical structure alone:

Anonymous: Chung lü, Hsi ch'un lai, no title. (YJHLC, p. 97; CYSC,
p. 1704)

1a   不能够歡會空能夠看
        (bû.) néng goù huōn huəì kūng néng (goù) kàn   xpxtppt *r*
        We can't meet in joy, all I can do is look at you,

b   沒亂煞心腸受用煞眼
        (mù.)[22] luòn shaì siə̄m chiáng shoù iùng (shaì) ân   xtppttp r
        It's distress to the heart for the joys of the eye.

c   一番相見一番難
        î. fān siāng gièn î. fān nán   xpxttpp r
        Once to meet is once to suffer;

2a   幾步間
        gî bù gàn   xts r
        A few steps apart

b   如隔萬重山
        riú gaî. vàn chúng shān   xttpp r
        Is like a wall of ten thousand mountains.

In the first two lines, substantives, verbs, and particles are kept
parallel. The particles are so distinctively colloquial that their use
as parallel elements gives the line a special colloquial flavor which
is even more satisfying because the structure is obvious and gives
the impression of "coming out right." Of all the aspects of colloquial
verse the most universally appealing is the impression that ordinary
words of common speech fall easily into noticeable patterns. It overrides faults in treatment of subject matter, repetitiousness, and lack
of pithiness. It is the divine spark of folk song.

From the free forms of parallelism, it is only a step to arbitrary
patterns of repetition. We have seen that san-ch'ü writers were fond
of creating sound patterns whenever possible, adding extra rhymes
and developing effects with assonance and alliteration, and it is natural that they also strove for effects with arbitrary repetition of larger

----

22. 沒 is omitted in YJHLC. It serves here as a particle of emphasis.

groups of sounds, phrases, and lines. Often these were suggested by the shape of the verse form, as in the hsi-ch'ü, Hsiao ho-shang, in which three tieh-tzu must be used at the head of every line, or as in songs like the Tao-tao ling and Shan p'o yang[23] in whose final lines there are special patterns resembling refrains. There are signs of rhetorical excellence in spontaneous patterns reenforcing meaning and emotional effect but often they become tours de force with little but consistency to recommend them.

One simple form repeats the same word in every line of a poem, extending its meaning, sometimes making puns upon it. This often became a contest among writers who passed the time "sharing rhymes" or writing sequels. Lü Chi-min, in one of the better examples, does this cleverly with the two characters in the name of the courtesan to whom he dedicated the poem:[24]

Lü Chi-min (fl. 1302): Shuang tiao, Che kuei ling, "Tseng yü-hsiang, To Jade-fragrance." (YJHLC, p. 307; CYSC, p. 1155)

1 可人兒暖玉生香
   kô riə́n (f̄) nuôn iừ. shə̄ng hiāng   xpxtpp r
   The beauty is warm jade radiating fragrance;

2a 弄玉團香
    lừng iừ. tuốn hiāng   xtpp r
    Dally with jade, dally with fragrance;

 b 惜玉憐香
    sî. iừ. liə́n hiāng   xtpp r
    Love the jade, love the fragrance!

3a 畫蛾眉玉鑑遺香
    (huà ó məî) iừ. gām í hiāng   xtpp r
    After she paints her eyebrows the mirror of
        jade is touched with fragrance;

 b 伴才郎玉枕留香
    (buồn tsaí láng) iừ. zhiə̄m lioú hiāng   xtpp r
    When she's been with her lover, her pillow
        of jade[25] is tinged with fragrance.

---

23. For an example of the last, see pp. 122—23.

24. For other examples, see Kuan Han-ch'ing's Yi chih hua, quoted in Chapter 1, p. 37; Kuan Yün-shih's Ch'ing chiang yin entitled "Li ch'un," (YJHLC, p. 359; CYSC, p. 371) in which the word "spring" as well as one of the five elements is used in each line; Chang Yang-hao's Sai hung ch'iu, YJHLC, p. 10, CYSC, p. 427; Jen Yü's Hsiao liang chou, YJHLC, pp. 16—17, CYSC, p. 1005.

25. Not a pillow in the western sense but a jade headrest.

4a   捧酒卮玉容噴香
    pûng dzioû zhī iù. iúng pə̀n hiāng   xtx, xptx r
    When she holds out the wine cup, her jade
        visage breathes a fragrance,

b   摘花枝玉指偷香
    zhaî. huā zhī iù. zhī toū hiāng   xpp, xtpp r
    When plucking the flower, her fingers of
        jade steal the fragrance.

5a   問玉何香
    və̀n iù. hó hiāng   xtpp r
    What is jade's fragrance?

b   料玉多香
    liaù iù. duō hiāng   xtpp *r*
    I'd say jade has much fragrance.

c   見玉思香
    gièn iù. sz̄ hiāng   xtpp *r*
    Seeing jade I think of fragrance,

d   買玉尋香
    maî iù. siə́m hiāng   xtpp r
    When buying jade I look for fragrance.

    Such consistent use of this device usually sounds clever and friv-
olous but T'ao Yüan-ming (b. 365) repeated similarly the verb "to
stop" in his "Poem on Giving up Drink" yet managed to avoid frivol-
ity.[26]
    In the following poem, Kuan Yün-shih demonstrates with imagina-
tion and originality how repetition patterns may be used to control
subject matter:

Kuan Yün-shih (1286–1324): Chung lü, Hung hsiu hsieh, no title.
(YJHLC, p. 54; CYSC, pp. 363–64)

1a   挨着靠着雲窗同坐
    aī (zhio.) kaù (zhio.) iuə́n chuáng túng dzuò   xtxpsc r
    Caressing, cuddling, we sit together by the
        misty window,[27]

b   偎着抱着月枕雙歌
    uəì (zhio.) baù (zhio.) iuè. zhiə̂m shuāng gō   xpxtpp r
    Nestling, embracing, we sing together on the
        moonlit pillow.

---

    26. T'ao Yuan-ming, *T'ao yüan-ming chi*, iii, pp. 22a–b.
    27. *iuə́n chuāng* "cloud window"—the image suggests seclusion.

2   聽着數着怕着愁着早四更過
ti̅ng (zhio.) shù (zhio.) pà (zhio.) choú[28] (zhio.
       dzaû) sż ga̅ng guō   xtxptpp r
Listening, counting, fearful and anxious, so soon
    the fourth watch is past.

3a   四更過情未足
(sż ga̅ng guō) tsia̅ng və̀ dziû.   ptt
Fourth watch past, our love is not content,

b   情未足夜如梭
(tsia̅ng və̀ dziû.) iè riú suō   tpp r
Love uncontent, the night has flown,[29]

4   天哪更閏一更兒妨甚麼
(tien nà ga̅ng riuə́n) i̅. ga̅ng (f̌) fàng shiə̂m muō[30]   xpxcs r
O Heaven! What could it harm to add one
    extra hour?[31]

The first three lines are dominated by the verb phrases whose form
is the same throughout: a verb with full metrical value followed by a
grammatical particle that is extrametrical. The first two lines, parallel in construction, describe the two young lovers, blissful in their
lack of concern over the passing of time. The rhythm, at least in a
recitation of these lines, is even and gives no hint of anxiousness.
When the first striking of the fourth watch is heard, however, the
caresses and the songs they sing together are interrupted, they are
caught unawares and their surprise that time could have slipped by so
quickly gives way to disappointment and anxiety that they may be
discovered. The line introducing these feelings has a different structure, being a seven-syllable line whereas the preceding two are each
six-syllable lines. Four terse verb phrases in succession, each of
the same form as those in the previous lines and each expressing a
separate idea, make the substance of sentence 2. Four such phrases
increase considerably the rhythmic tension of the line and in this way
add to the emotional intensity that develops so suddenly in the scene.
There follows a chainlike repetition in which the last syllables in one

---

28. The *Hsin chiao chiu chüan pen* YCPH has *choú zhió. pà zhió.*
I follow the YCPH because the tones fit better. See the note on this
poem in CYSC, p. 364.
29. *iè riú suō* "night like a shuttle." The quickness of time is
usually compared to the weaver's shuttle.
30. A better ending to this line would have been in the pattern
pcs.
31. More accurately, "add one more watch," which would amount
to about two hours.

line become the first of the next. This makes lines 3a—b move briskly, and because the repeated phrases are, in addition, extrametrical syllables, the rhythm will have been the more taut when the song was sung. In recitation these phrases take on the character of four short lines; their final syllables develop the rhyme scheme *abba*, accentuating this abrupt phrasing much more than rhyme schemes like *aaaa* or *abab*.

Far from merely ornamenting the poem, the patterns of repetition as used by Kuan Yün-shih express an idea with the greatest possible clarity and force. This is especially admirable in view of the tendency among writers to overuse attractive rhetorical devices. Obviously the poem would have been quite different if Kuan Yün-shih had felt compelled to use the chainlike pattern[32] in every line so commonly used by other writers.

Beyond ornamenting a text, therefore, parallelism and patterns of repeated phrases enhance, even create, the significant ideas of a poem. That parallelism was perfected in other poetic genre restricted its use in san-ch'ü but little. This freedom to go beyond the restrictions of literary verse did not necessarily mean that san-ch'ü writers came immediately to show greater brilliance and imaginativeness in their use of parallelism, and the same is true of arbitrary forms of phrase repetition. It is clear, however, that a special kind of talent was necessary to use these devices to the best effect, and such talent sets the poet apart from other writers no matter whether he writes shih, tz'u, or san-ch'ü.

---

32. See also the anonymous Hsin shui ling, no title, the last song in the t'ao-shu, *Hsin chiao chiu chüan pen* YCPH, 2,v:177, or CYSC, p. 1846. Also Ch'iao Chi's Hsiao t'ao hung, YJHLC, p. 384, and CYSC, p. 588, among others.

5

Figures of Speech and Miscellaneous Rhetorical Devices

When dealing with the figure of speech in san-ch'ü, one is confronted with a twofold task: the need to explain the nature of figures that occur in san-ch'ü, and, born of this, the need to define and classify all types of figures of speech. My classification does not make wide use of traditional terms; instead, the names are derived from the conditions and relationships that presented themselves in the limited sphere of the poetry studied.

The term "figuration" refers to a use of language that purposely evokes senses or images different from those thought normal or literal. The imagery is evoked through language that becomes illusory by creating aberrations in the usual perceptions of reality and so seems to put actual things into unusual and illuminating perspectives. These perspectives can go unappreciated because of mental resistance to unusual associations, especially of things within our practical experience, but if we are led unawares, so that habits of mind do not interfere, the impression of unusual associations can be very strong. For example, a mirror can create for us unusual space relationships which, to our amusement or dismay, confuse our normal sight perceptions. We call this optical illusion. Similarly, the puzzle of Zeno[1] might be called a mathematical illusion because, given the condition of fixed time, it makes a perfectly logical but obviously "incorrect" representation of reality. It is exactly in this way that a figure of speech is a grammatical illusion which leads us to draw conclusions about reality that the mind would resist were it not guided by the shape of the language in which the idea is expressed.

---

1. In which Achilles, even though he could run ten times as fast, could never pass the tortoise providing it was given a head start.

In the following analysis of grammatical illusion, or figure of speech, the figures are divided into two classes: (1) *comparison*, in which two terms, usually substantives, are compared in an utterance through one of various ways; (2) *substitution*, in which we find a figurative term in an utterance substituted for a more usual or proper term.[2]

All figures of speech are, in a manner of speaking, substitutions, that is to say, a figurative term standing in place of a proper term which is never expressed. What distinguishes the two classes is a kind of redundance that underlies all comparisons. The statement, "The grass is like grass," has limited descriptive value and invites a figurative term such as "a carpet" or the like to stand in the place of the reference to grass in general. It is characteristic of comparisons that the proper term, "grass" (general) in the example, even though not expressed, is synonymous with another word in the utterance, "grass" (specific) in the example, and that it is between the synonym and the figurative term that figurative activity is generated. In the substitution figure, on the other hand, there is in the utterance an obviously "wrong" word, and figurative activity is generated between it and what we feel should be the "right" word, as in the example "joy lives here" meaning "my beloved lives here," the proper term "my beloved" having no synonym elsewhere in the statement.[3]

In either of these classes figures are liable to banality; the classifications do not imply that one type is intrinsically more striking or revelational than another. In the analysis of figures one is constantly reminded of the balance that must be struck between how tight or lax is syntax structure and how natural or forced, within the literary conventions, is the association between the things related. This balance, assuring on the one hand comprehensibility, and on the other, freshness and lively imagery, is basic to the success of all figures of speech. It should be understood at this point also that speech figures do not have the importance in Chinese rhetoric that metaphor holds in European languages. Parallelism in Chinese takes a more prominent position.

We shall begin by discussing simple figures—first comparison and its forms, second the many types of simple substitution—and conclude with a few remarks on complex figures.

---

2. For "figurative term" and "proper term," as well as for many other useful ideas, I am indebted to Christine Brooke-Rose's *A Grammar of Metaphor*.

3. A clear distinction between these two classes, comparison and substitution, is confused by the term "metaphor," for in its normal usage metaphor includes some comparisons as well as most types of the substitution figure.

Comparison figures, as we said before, are made between the figurative term and a synonym of the proper term. For convenience we
shall call the synonym and the figurative term the elements of the
comparison. As the copula is not always needed in grammatical equa-
tions in Chinese, it is reasonable from a stylistic point of view to
draw a distinction between the two ways of linking the elements. The
class of figures by comparison, therefore, has two types: (a) expressed
comparisons, whose elements are linked by a word of comparison or
equation; and (b) implied comparisons in which the comparison is
made through juxtaposition of the elements compared.

Although an analogy might be drawn here to metaphor and simile,
it is of little advantage to introduce Western distinctions, especially
since they bring with them conventional prejudgments, and similes
seem not to have the prestige of metaphors. Just as one cannot say
that one word, per se, is poetic and another is not, the expressed
comparison is not necessarily of less aesthetic value than other types
of figures. It has its special advantages which are well illustrated in
the second two lines of this quatrain by Kuan Han-ch'ing:

Kuan Han-ch'ing: Cheng kung, Pai ho-tzu, no title. (YJHLC, p. 23;
CYSC, p. 155)[4]

1a 四時春富貴
    sż shf́ chiuə̄n fὺ guəỉ   xpptt
    Of the four seasons, Spring is richest and noblest,

 b 萬物酒風流
    vàn vὺ. dzioû fūng lioú   xttpp r
    Of all things, wine the most liberating,

2a 澄澄水如藍
    chiə́ng chiə́ng shuəî riú lám   xttpp
    Clear, clear, the water is like sorrel,

 b 灼灼花如繡
    zhiaû. zhiaû. huā riú sioù   xtppt r
    Bright, bright, the flowers like brocade.

There is here a feeling of ancient poetry which stems in part from
the choice of vocabulary but also from the artless quality of the figures. The expressed comparison, having such explicit form, can be
used in frank or ingenuous speech, sometimes with stark effect, sometimes, as here, with simplicity.

---

4. In the TPYF, iii, p. 4b, and the CYSC this is the first of four
quatrains. In both Luo K'ang-lieh, *Pei hsiao-ling wen-tzu p'u*, and
YJHLC they are grouped as two eight-line songs. For present purposes
I take them as quatrains.

The expressed comparison takes a variety of forms. The comparisons in lines 3b and 3c by Ah-li Hsi-ying have the same structure as those above but the elements in them have a slightly more complex form:

Ah-li Hsi-ying (fl. 1320): Shuang tiao, Tien ch'ien huan, "Lan yün wo, The Haunt of Idle Clouds."[5]

1a 懶雲窩
lân iuə́n uō   tpp r
In the Haunt of Idle Clouds

  b 醒時詩酒醉時歌
siə̄ng shŕ shī dzioû dzuə̀ì shŕ gō   xpxttpp r
It's poems and wine when I'm sober and
    singing when I'm drunk.

2a 瑤琴不理拋書臥
iaú kiə́m bû. lî paū shiū uò   xpxtppt r
The lute is out of tune, I toss aside my books
    and sleep

  b 無夢南柯
vú mùng nám kō   xtpp r
Without dreams of ambition.[6]

3a 得清閑儘快活
(dəî.) tsiə̄ng hán dziə̄n kuaî huó.   xpxtp r
I have peace and leisure and unlimited happiness;

  b 日月似擲梭過
(rì. iuè. sz̀) tsuōn suō guò   ppt r
The sun and moon are like the thrown shuttle passing,

  c 富貴比花開落
fù guə̀ì (bî) huā koī luò.   xtppt r
Wealth and honor, like flowers blooming and falling.

4a 青春去也
tsiə̄ng chiuə̄n kiù iê   pptt
Spring is passing!

  b 不樂如何
bû. luò. riú hó   xtpp r
If you don't enjoy life, what then?

---

5. TPYF, i, p. 15b. The version in YJHLC, p. 272 differs considerably from that in the TPYF. See CYSC, p. 339.

6. The reference is to the T'ang story "Nan-k'o chi" which is the most famous of a type of story in which life and one's ambitions are all shown as a dream.

In expressed comparisons of the pattern, "A is like B," A and B
are usually both nouns; Ah-li Hsi-ying's lines equate a noun with a
noun clause. The two figures compare, in line 3b, the movement of
the sun and moon with the passing of the shuttle, and in line 3c, the
activity of getting rich and having title with the life cycle of a flower.
Neither comparison is very fresh but they are somewhat more vivid
than a noun to noun comparison like "moon" and "shuttle." If the
signs of comparison, *s̀z* and *bî*, were left out of these lines, the style
would be more elegant.

Expressed comparisons have a complex form that introduces an
adjective through which both elements of the figure are indirectly
compared. They take the form "A is (or has) as much (or more, or less)
x than B." The negative form is used in this line from Chang K'o-
chiu's poem cited below:

比人心山未險

(bî) riə́n siə̂m shān vəì hiêm
Compared to men's hearts, mountains
     were never dangerous.

The pattern "compared to A, B has no x" is an inversion, with hyperbole, of "B has less x than A." This form seems to require exaggera-
tion to avoid the anticlimax of a statement like "compared to men's
hearts, mountains are not dangerous." The inversion and the fact that
vəì is a bit more emphatic than *bù.* are to the poet's credit.

Implied comparisons, we will recall, have no linking words by
which the relationships between the two elements in a comparative
figure are made. The first two lines in the next poem are good examples of this type:

Chang K'o-chiu: Chung lü, Hung hsiu hsieh, "T'ien-t'ai p'u-pu ssu,
The Waterfall Temple at T'ien-t'ai." (YJHLC, p. 56; CYSC, p. 798)

1a 絕頂峯攢雪劍
     dziué. diə̂ng fūng tsuón siuê. gièm   xtxp sc r
     At their very tops the peaks gather like swords
          of snow,

b 懸崖水挂冰簾
     hiến aí shuəî guà biə̄ng liém   xpxtpp r
     On the sheer cliff the stream hangs like a curtain
          of ice.

2 倚樹哀猿弄雲尖
     ĭ shiù oĭ iuén lùng iuə́n dziēm   xtxptpp r
     In the trees, monkeys[7] play with the tops of clouds;

_____

7. *oĭ iuén* "wailing gibbons" is, in verse, a conventional term for
"monkeys," like "bright moon" for "moon."

3a   血華啼杜宇
     (hiê. huá) tî dù iû   ptt *r*
     Among the blood flowers the cuckoo calls,[8]

 b   陰洞吼飛廉
     (iə̄m dùng) hoû fəī liém   tpp   r
     From dark caves the wind-god howls ...

4   比人心山未險
     (bî) rián siə̄m shān vəī hiêm   xpxcs r
     Compared to men's hearts, mountains hold
        no peril.

The structure of the figures in lines 1a and 1b is the same, so we
need analyze only the first line, which we may translate as follows:

        Very top peaks gather snow swords.[9]

The figure lies in the last four words. There can be no verb-object
link between "gather" and "swords" as the English word order suggests; the relationship is instead a comparison in which peaks are
described as swords. Whether the peaks are swords or are like swords
is relevant to English construction and style; the similes in the translation keep the elements of the figure together better than metaphors
do. Still it is reasonable to say that the copula could convey the impact of the original just as well. The Chinese text sets out three
facts; the lack of grammatical particles produces a conciseness of
which the expressed comparison in English or Chinese would not be
capable.
    Implied comparisons are not infrequent in san-ch'ü nor are they al-
ways confined to one line. The following poem is a good illustration
of extended comparison used to gain heightened imagery:

Anonymous: Chung lü, Hung hsiu hsieh, no title. (YJHLC, p. 64;
CYSC, p. 1695)

1a   窗外雨聲聲不住
     chuā̄ng uaì iû shiā̄ng (shiā̄ng) bû. zhiù   xtxpsc r
     Outside the window rain sounds ceaselessly,

_____

    8. The azalea, said to have gotten its red color from the cuckoo who
sings until it spits blood. The cuckoo's mournful call, according to
tradition, sounds like the Chinese phrase "better to return home," and
is associated with the sadness of parted lovers or of those far from home
    9. This particular line reads easily in a 3-3 syntax pattern but in
the Hung hsiu hsieh verse form it is nearly always 2-2-2 (or in the
case of seven syllables, 3-4, i.e., 1-2-2-2), and does not allow three
syllables after the caesura.

b   枕邊泪點點長吁
     zhiâm biên luəì diêm (diêm) chiáng hiū   xpxtpp   r
     Beside my pillow tears fall with my sighs.

2   雨聲泪點急相逐
     iū shiāng luəì diêm gî. siāng zhiú.   xtxptpp   r
     Sounding rain, falling tears urge on one another;

3a   雨聲兒添悽惨
     (iū shiāng f) tiēm tsî tsâm   ptt
     The rain sound adds to grief,

b   泪點兒助長吁
     (luəì diêm f) zhù chiáng hiū   tpp   r
     Teardrops provoke more sighs.

4   枕邊泪到多如窗外雨
     (zhiâm biên luəì daù) duō riú chuāng uaì iū   xpxcs   r
     As many tears are by my pillow as rain outside
       my window.

The relationship between rain and tears is first suggested in lines
1a and 1b, but only indirectly through parallelism. Sentence 2 makes
the association clearer but makes no direct link between the two elements. The following two lines, 3a–b, show teardrops and the sound
of rain to have the same effect on the grief of the speaker in the poem,
but it is not until the final line that a direct comparison is made. It
then appears as a hyperbole in which the amount of tears is compared
with the amount of rain. Beyond parallel structure and the comparison
in the last line, no links are needed to make the comparison strong
and consistent. An association between tears and rain is quite obvious, to be sure, but the poem evokes concrete similarities that are
fresh, and this is the basis for originality in figurative language.

Substitution, the second class into which simple figures of speech
fall, covers a large field which can be divided into the following
types: (*a*) attributive substitutions, (*b*) verb substitutions, (*c*) noun
substitutions, (*d*) allegories, (*e*) inversions, (*f*) fabrications. The last
three are actually special cases of one or more of the other types, but
because they are so widely used, they deserve separate discussion.
The attributive substitution itself takes different forms, namely, describing attributives or specifying attributives.

The describing attributive is what traditional rhetoric calls a colorful adjective, but I prefer to consider it in the level of figurative language because it conforms to the nature of substitution figures and
can create heightened imagery in the hands of imaginative writers. The
first two lines of the poem that follows provide two examples of conventional though good describing attributives:

Ch'iao Chi: Nan lü, Ssu k'uai yü, "Yung shou, Hands." (YJHLC, p. 164; CYSC, p. 575)

1a 玉掌溫
    iù. zhiâng uə̄n   xxp *r*
    Her jade hands warm,

  b 瓊枝嫩
     kiə̂ng zhī̄ nuə̀n   ppt r
     Her coral fingers soft;

2a 閑弄閑拈暗生春
    hân lùng hân niêm ò̀m shə̄ng chiuə̄n   xtpptpp r
    Toying idly, fondling idly, stirs the secret passions,

  b 為纖柔長惹風流恨
     (uə̀) siêm rioú zhiâng riê fū̄ng lioú hə̀n   xpxtppt r
     Their graceful tenderness rouses love's regrets;

3a 掠翠鬟
    liò. tsuə̀ piə̂n   xtp
    She grooms her dark eyebrows,

  b 整鬢雲
     zhiə̂ng gì iuə̂n   xtp r
     Smoothes the cloudy chignon;

  c 可喜損
     kô hî suə̀n   xtp[10] r
     So pretty it's devastating.

There is an abundance of describing attributives in san-ch'ü, most of them occurring before the noun as in the example above. They are found to occur in the predicate as well; the excerpt below has two examples (full text on pp. 122−23):

         峯巒如聚
         fū̄ng luô̂n riú dziù
         Peaks as if massed,

         波濤如怒
         buō taú riú nù
         Waves as if angry . . .

The predicate attributive in Chinese may occur without *riú* or any other linking word. In fact, all noun modifiers in the predicate and verbs not followed by another word can function as predicate attribu-

---

10. Although a p'ing tone appears more frequently at the end of this line, a shang tone is allowed.

tives and can become figurative language. In spite of this, figurative
constructions with the attributive in the predicate are not very common.

A special type of describing attributive is the classifier which
when substituted properly can make very effective figures of speech.
The classifier is a grammatical device as commonplace in Chinese
as the article "a" is in English, yet it is as precise and concrete in
its description of a noun as the phrase "a pound of flesh." Classi-
fiers effectively guide the reader's attention to the desired aspect of
the noun, as in the phrases *î. zhiən iēn*—陣煙 "a puff of smoke," or
î. liû iēn—縷煙 "a wisp of smoke." By their nature they are "practical metaphors," but used as in line 2a below they easily achieve the
freshness or the illuminating perspectives requisite to good figures
of speech:

Kuan Yün-shih: Shuang tiao, Ch'ing chiang yin, "Hsi pieh, No. 1,
Parting." (YJHLC, p. 358; CYSC, p. 370)

la 窗間月娥風韻煞
    chuāng gān iuè. ó fūng iuən shâ.[11]   xptppcs r
    How lovely by the window is the goddess of
        the moon,

 b 良夜千金價
    liáng iè tsiēn giəm gà   xtppc r
    The beautiful night is worth a thousand pieces
        of gold,

2a 一掬可憐情
    î. giû. kô lién tsiáng   xpxtp
    A touch of pity . . .

 b 幾句臨明話
    gî giù liəm miáng huà   xtppt r
    A few words before dawn,

3   小書生這歇兒難立馬
    (siaû) shiū shəng zhiê hiê. (ŕ)[12] nán lì. mâ   xptppcs r
    This time it is difficult for the young scholar
        to leave.

It is an excellent example showing how a poet can broaden the
connotations of a noun without adding to the bulk of the statement.
The classifier *giû.* usually refers to what one might scoop up in the

---

11. 煞 is given only as *shai* in the CYYY.
12. Although *ŕ* is extrametrical, it must have affected the tone of
the previous syllable. For a similar instance, see Chapter 1, p. 29.

hand, such as water from a pond. Substituting "a handful" for a
proper term meaning "a little bit" evokes special imagery on its own,
but there is another factor that throws light on the noun "feeling";
"a handful" in addition to its literal meaning has connotations from
its frequent use in the expression "a handful of tears." This must
have been in Kuan Yün-shih's mind when he wrote the line.

Kuan Han-ch'ing achieves a special subtlety with the classifier
in line 2a of the following poem:

Kuan Han-ch'ing: Nan lü, Ssu k'uai yü, "Pieh ch'ing, Sorrow of Parting." (YJHLC, p. 160; CYSC, p. 156)

1a   自送別
     dzż sùng bié.   xxp r
     Since the farewell,

  b 心難捨
     siə̄m nán shiê   ppt r
     In my heart I cannot let you go.

2a   一點相思幾時絕
     î. diêm siāng sż gî shŕ dziué.   xtpptpp r
     When do even meager longings end?

  b 凭闌袖掃楊花雪
     piə́ng lán sioù fû. iáng huā siuê.   xpxtppt r
     I lean over the railing, my sleeves brush the
          snowy willow-down.

3a   溪又斜
     kī ioù sié   xtp r
     The stream winds away,

  b 山又遮
     shān ioù zhiē   xtp r
     A hill screens the view,

  c 人去也
     riə́n kiù iê   xtp r
     And you are gone.

     In line 2a the classifier î. diêm "a dot" is unusual for the noun
siāng sż "longing"; one would expect the more conventional "thread"
which is derived from a well-established pun on sż "longing" with
the homophone sż "silk, thread." The verb dziué. "to break" at the
end of the line is more consistent with the thread image. Although
both the classifier and the verb have a range of meanings broad
enough to be consistent with one another, on closer examination their
imagery is enough at variance to create interesting reverberations in

the line. There is first the suggestion in *gî shǐ dziuế*. "when will it end?" of the speaker's impatience to be done with so painful a longing; in that context *î. diêm* suggests the sharpness of concentration of the longing. At the same time this question "when will it end (or break)?" is a poignantly simple statement of wonder: how can something so fragile as longing or love be so constant, being drawn out like a thin thread over great time and distance? This arises from the concrete sense of *dziuế*, which means to break as a thread breaks; *î. diêm* then emphasizes the fragility of the love between two people who must be separated.

Unlike the describing attributives above, which modify a literal noun, the specifying attributive indicates that the noun it modifies is to be taken in a symbolic sense or is a figure of speech itself. Note Ch'iao Chi's line

脱這金枷玉鎖
tuô. zhiê giəm gā iù. suô
Escape the golden cangue and lock of jade.[13]

The cangue and lock are fetters from which one might try to escape literally but the adjectives make it clear that these are no ordinary fetters but the bonds of human existence. If the expression is very popular, specifying attributives sometimes are not essential to understanding the line. Although this is true of the cangue and lock, which are popular in Buddhist symbolism, references to fetters in their literal sense are commonplace enough to cause some confusion if a specifying attributive is not used.

Substitutions of verbs do not occur as frequently as attributive substitutions. There is one such figure by Chang K'o-chiu in line 3b below (full text on p. 93):

3a   遊魚翻凍影
(ioú iú) fān dùng iəng
The swimming fish flicker the cool shadows,

b   啼鳥犯春聲
(tǐ niaû) fàn chiuən shiəng
The singing birds assault the sounds of spring,

4   落梅香暮景
luô. məǐ hiāng mù giəng
The fallen plum blossoms make the evening
     fragrant.

---

13. Nan-lü, Yü chiao chih. (YJHLC, p. 180; CYSC, p. 576). It is the eighth line in the first of two untitled songs. YJHLC does not have *tuô.* at the head of the line.

It is only the verb "assault"[14] that replaces a proper term, "add to" or "create," and so can stand as a figure of speech, but the verbs in the other two lines are used well and create vivid imagery also. It is appropriate to remark here that in duscussions of style the limits between "colorful" uses of literal terms and figures of speech can be at best vague and the effects created by the grammatical illusion are often equaled in vividness and power by literal utterance, as the example well illustrates.

Noun substitutions present certain problems because nouns are associated most often with concrete referents that are less easily shifted into new perspectives than abstract qualities or actions. Highly original noun substitutions run the risk of being misunderstood or completely incomprehensible; those that are easily understood are likely to be banal.

In practice the poet may either substitute a noun of obvious or hackneyed associations with a proper term, or use a designating attributive. Being forced to rely on hackneyed associations of nouns does not deter the writer of san-ch'ü, but in the previous example by Chang K'o-chiu some interpretations of line 3b might take "spring sounds" to refer to the spring atmosphere, which is a noun substitution of a sort not quite so obvious. In line 1b of Chang K'o-chiu's poem (p. 93)

玉釣垂翠竹閒亭

(iù.) goū chuəí tsuəì zhiû. hán tiə̌ng
The crescent moon hangs over green
    bamboo by the quiet pavilion . . .

he uses the well-worn figure "hook" to stand for the crescent moon. Even though it is a poetic cliché, it always occurs with the adjective "jade," a designating attributive of the kind we saw earlier, which keeps the reader from making literal associations with the noun.

Once a noun substitution is established, it can easily be extended to function as an allegory. It was with such an extension that Ma Chih-yüan, in line 1a below, considerably enlivened the hackneyed association between a mirror and the moon:

Ma Chih-yüan: Hsien lü, Shang hua shih, "Chü shui yüeh tsai shou, Cupping up Water, the Moon is in My Hands," the first song of the set. (CYSC, p. 255)[15]

---

14. There is a variant 泛 which is probably a better reading in this context, but see CYSC, p. 800 n. The line, translated "the singing birds make the spring sounds overflow," still has a figure of speech.

15. The titles for this set and the set that follows it in the anthologies are two lines from "Ch'un shan ye yüeh" by Yü Liang-shih. See *Ch'üan t'ang shih*, p. 1659.

1a 　古鏡當天秋正磨
　　gû giàng dāng tiēn tsioū zhiàng muó   xtppttp r
　　In autumn the ancient mirror against the sky
　　　　is newly polished.

b 　玉露瀼瀼寒漸多
　　iù. lù riáng riáng hón dzièm duō   xtppttp r
　　The dew is heavy, the cold increases;

2a 　星斗燦銀河
　　siōng doû tsàn iàn hó   pttpp r
　　Stars twinkle in the Milky Way,

b 　泉澄潦盡
　　tsiuén chiáng laû[16] dzièn   pptt
　　The spring water is clear as it drips away,

c 　仙桂影婆婆
　　siēn guaî iàng puó suō   xttpp r
　　The shadow of the fairy cassia[17] shimmers.

The figurative "mirror" shows the color, the shape, and the mellow-
ness of the moon, and although it is this word we read, it is the moon
on which our attention is focused. Ma Chih-yüan then turns our attention to the brightness of the moon, but using the verb *muó* "to
polish" he does so entirely in terms of the substituted noun. Now in
the phrase "a mirror newly polished," all the elements are related
literally, but because we understand that "mirror" actually stands for
something else, the whole line is moved out of the literal realm and
functions as an allegory—albeit a minute one.

The inversion, like the allegory, is a special kind of noun substitution. On the surface it appears to be a noun substitution of the
usual kind, but when a proper term is sought one finds none, and what
seemed to be the figurative term is in fact a literal sign of the referent; it is the rest of the statement that is figurative. Take for example the rather protracted personification in the following poem:

Hsieh Ang-fu (fl. 1302): Shuang tiao, Ch'u ti'en yao with Ch'ing
chiang yin, no title, only second strophe is quoted. (YJHLC, p. 376;
CYSC, p. 718)

1a 　春若有情應解語
　　chiuēn riò. ioû tsiáng iāng gaî iû   xptppcs r
　　If spring has feelings it should know how to talk,

---

16. Some editions have 源. See CYSC, p. 255 n.
17. It was believed that these trees grew on the moon.

b   問着無憑據

    vә̀n zhió. vú piә́ng giù   xtppc r

    But, asking, there is no answer.[18]

2a 江東日暮雲

    giā̄ng dū̄ng rì. mù iuә́n   xpxtp

    The evening clouds east of the River,

b   渭北春天樹

    uә̀ɪ bә̀ɪ. chiuә̄n tiē̄n shiù   xtppt r

    The spring trees north of the Wei;[19]

3   不知那答兒是春住處

    bū̀. zhī̄ nuó dā̀. (ɪ̃[20], shɪ̀) chiuә̀n zhiù chiù   xptppcs r

    I don't know where spring can be.

Spring can hardly be the figurative term as it is literally what the poet is talking about. On the other hand the statements about its having feelings and a place of abode are what generate the figurative activity. Therefore, instead of a statement with a figurative term imbedded in it, we have a literal term supported by a figurative statement.

The fabrication, the last type to be discussed under substitution figures, is similar to the inversion in that its proper term has an unusual function. Note the last line of this poem:

Kuan Yün-shih: Shuang tiao, Ch'ing chiang yin, "Hsi pieh, No. 3, Parting." (YJHLC, p. 358; CYSC, p. 370)

1a 湘雲楚雨歸路杳

    siā̄ng iuә́n chū̂ iū̂ guә̄ɪ lù iaū̂   xptppcs r

    The clouds of Hsiang, the rain of Ch'u, and
        the long way home,

b   總是傷懷抱

    dzū̂ng shɪ̀ shiā̄ng huaɪ̂ baù   xtppc r

    All break my heart;

2a 江聲攬暮濤

    giā̄ng shiә̄ng gaū̂ mù taū́   xpxtp *r*

    River sounds stir in the waves at dusk,

---

    18. Literally, "there is no evidence."

    19. Lines 2a–b are from Tu Fu's poem "On a Spring Day Thinking of Li Po"; *Ch'üan t'ang shih*, p. 1300. The lines suggest great distance separating two people.

    20. See Note 12 of this chapter.

    21. In YJHLC, 掩 is a misprint.

b   樹影留殘照
    shiừ iâng lioứ tsán zhiaừ   xtppt r
    And tree shadows hold the fading light;

3   蘭舟把愁都載了
    lán zhiou bâ choứ dū dzaì liaû   xptppcs r
    The boat[22] is loaded down with sorrow.

The poem describes the parting of two lovers, and the boat's pon-
derous movements suggest a reluctance to leave. It is as though the
boat were heavily loaded down, and the term "sorrow" seems to be a
straightforward substitution for "cargo." Unlike the other kinds of
figures in which the poet is trying to suggest a proper term, however,
this figure is not intended to describe any real cargo in this figure
of speech. If we take "sorrow" literally, as we did "spring" in Hsieh
Ang-fu's poem above, it is difficult to know what statement the poet
is making about sorrow, so the inversion does not fully explain the
workings of this figure of speech. The descriptive element in the
line is "the boat is loaded down" but the only thing one can say about
this phrase is that it is untrue, it is a fabrication used to heighten
imagery.

Up to this point we have considered as far as possible the forms
of simple figures of speech. We can now examine figurative constructions in which two or more simple figures are combined to make a
compound figure of speech. The most frequent compound is composed
of the designating attributive and another type, usually a noun substitution.
    The figures in lines 1a–b of Chang K'o-chiu's poem on T'ien-t'ai
Mountain are compounds that are comparisons of two elements with
a figurative attributive attached to each element (full text on pp. 107–8).

    絕頂峯攢雲劍
    dziué. diâng fūng tsuốn siuê. gièm
    At their very tops the peaks gather
       like swords of snow ...

The Chinese verb for "gather" makes a figure of speech when it modifies "peaks" but it is most often found to modify "swords." On the
other hand, "snow" is a figurative attributive of "swords" and most
often modifies "peaks." The poet reversed nouns and modifiers and
though it is altogether likely he did so to conform to the metrical pattern, it is creditable that he saw fit to let the line stand. It serves

---

22. lán zhiou "orchid boat" —merely a poetic reference to any
boat.

as one of the better examples of effects achieved by compounding of
figures. The elements become figurative variations on one another—
peaks that can be gathered are more like swords, and swords that
are of snow are more like peaks; the compounding serves to fuse the
elements into a single image.

Compound figures do not always have the result that the lines of
Chang K'o-chiu achieve, but more often they are used out of neces-
sity to clarify the noun substitution. Such is the first line in this
poem:

Ch'iao Chi: Shuang tiao, Shui hsien-tzu, "Ch'ung kuan p'u-pu, A
Waterfall Revisited." (YJHLC, p. 248; CYSC, p. 626)

1a 天機纖罷月梭閑

    tiēn gĭ zhî bà iuê. suō hán   xpxttpp r
    The loom of the sky has stopped working, the
       moon shuttle rests;

b 石壁高垂雪練寒

    shí. bî. gaō chuəí siuê. liên hón   xtppxtp r
    The stone cliff hovers, the silk-like snow is cold,

c 冰絲帶雨懸霄漢

    biəng sź daì iû hién siaū hòn   xpxtppt r
    Threads of ice carrying rain hang from the sky;

2a 幾千年曬未乾

    (gî) tsiēn nién shaì vəì gōn   ppxcs r
    It will never dry up in a thousand years,

b 露華涼人怯衣單

    (lù) huá liáng riên kiê. ĭ dān   ppxtpp r
    The dew is cold and I quail in my thin clothes,

3a 似白虹飲澗

    (sź) baí. húng (iəm) gàn   ppt *r*
    It is like a white rainbow drinking at a stream,

b 玉龍下山

    (iù.) liúng hà shān   xts r
    Like a jade dragon descending the mountain,

c 晴雪飛灘

    tsiə́ng siuê. fəī tān   xtpp r
    And like snow by the river bank flying under a
       clear sky.

The basis for the line is an allegory in which the sky and moon
are represented by the terms "loom" and "shuttle." Because the terms
on their own are ambiguous, each has a specifying attributive. The

term and its attributive together make a separate figure of speech.
The attributives themselves do not refer directly to heaven and the
moon because they are subordinate to the nouns "loom" and "shuttle,"
nor, if they were changed into nouns themselves, could they support
the allegory. In both "loom" and "shuttle" figures, the two words in
figurative relationship are used to do the work of one literal term;
the adjective changes the semantic reference of the noun, the noun
both indicates grammatical function and provides the point of depart-
ure for the allegory.

One other example of compound figure will suffice. In the line we
met previously in the discussion of both verb substitutions and noun
substitutions (see pp. 93, 113).

啼鳥犯春聲

tí niaû fàn chiuān shiāng
The singing birds assault the sounds of
    spring (i.e., spring atmosphere)...

both the verb and its object may be taken as figurative terms; that is
to say, each replaces a term that more properly signifies the referent.
Because of their grammatical relationship, however, the meanings can
reverberate in a great variety of ways, at least in theory. There is
the relationship between the figurative verb "assault" and the object
"sounds," between the proper terms of the verb and object "create"
and "atmosphere" between the figurative verb "assault" and proper
object "atmosphere," and between the proper verb "create" and figurative object "sounds." Not all these relationships are likely to pre-
vail in a single reading, certainly not with the same intensity. In
the example, the verb "assault" is most likely to be adjusted in the
mind to accommodate "spring sounds." If we take the variant 浸,
which occurs in some texts and which means "to flood," the object is
more likely to undergo adjustment and the verb to stand as it is in the
line. Much depends upon historical and current usage in determining
which word will retain its literal associations and which will be forced
into figurative associations.[23]

Miscellaneous rhetorical devices are a varied group and could be
discussed indefinitely but here we will consider only three in particular: allusion, cliché, and the treatment of detail.

Allusions fall into two broad classes: (a) the literary allusion, or
the borrowing of phrases or lines from another work, and (b) the historical allusion which includes popular legends, both the scholarly

---

23. The term whose associations with its referent are clearest is
the one most likely to resist figurative interpretations. The nature of
such associations would make a most interesting study.

and popular views of history as well as references to geographical terms. By alluding to well-known lines of verse, to historical or legendary situations, characters, or places, a writer is not only able to achieve a special brevity of expression, but can with some certainty govern the attitudes his poem will arouse in his readers.

Literary allusion often gives the appearance of an attempted show of erudition; when used most effectively, however, the borrowed phrase makes a direct link with the source, which if it is well known enough, brings its meanings and its mood to the new poem. This happens in lines 2a-b of Hsieh Ang-fu's poem on spring (see p. 116), but the last line of Chang K'o-chiu's poem (see p. 108) seems merely to use the idea as a random ending to his verse. Compare his line

比人心山未險
(bî) riə́n siə̄m shān vəî hiêm
Compared to men's hearts, mountains
    hold no peril.

with these by Yung T'ao (fl. 846):

楚客莫言山勢險
ch'u k'o muo yen shan shih hsien
The traveller of Ch'u should not say
    the mountains are dangerous,
世人心更險于山
shih jen hsin keng hsien yu shan
The heart of man in the world is more
    dangerous than mountains.[24]

Yung T'ao is making a comment on the state of man. If we recall the rest of Chang's poem we will see that his concluding line is outstanding neither as an allusion to Yung T'ao's or any similar statement about man, nor as a line especially pertinent to the description of the waterfall on T'ien-t'ai.

Historical allusions appear in several of the verses quoted earlier. We saw in the poem written to the girl with a mole on her cheek (p. 60) how a situation could be described entirely in terms of legend. The allusion raised the poem's literary value because it not only allowed concise expression, but, through the analogy to the antics of royal personages, it made a commonplace situation universally interesting. The result one can achieve with allusions are infinite. The poet Wang Ting has achieved excellent satire by alluding to one of the popular love stories of his time. The actual events of the story

---

24. This poem is not included in the *Ch'üan t'ang shih*. These lines are cited from the *P'ei wen yün fu* under the entry *shan hsien* 山險 The readings are modern Chinese, using Wade-Giles.

vary but they usually revolve around a poor scholar, Shuang Chien, who is in love with the courtesan Su Ch'ing. Being poor, he has no means of buying Su Ch'ing from the brothel. After a long fruitless wait, Su Ch'ing, according to most versions, finally accepts the proposals of Feng K'uei, a wealthy but boorish tea merchant, and forsakes Shuang Chien. Yü-chang in Wang Ting's poem is the place of elopement, and where Shuang Chien in most versions of the story pursues the tea merchant's boat to look for Su Ch'ing.[25] Most allusions to the affair of Shuang Chien and Su Ch'ing emphasize the poignant theme of ideal love thwarted by crassness. Wang Ting derives humor by irreverently alluding to the ideal lovers in a poem about an amorous fat couple:

Wang Ting: Shuang tiao, P'o pu tuan, "P'ang fu ch'i, Fat Couple."
(YJHLC, p. 204; CYSC, p. 46)

la   一箇胖雙郎
     (î. go) pàng shuāng láng   tpp r
     A fat Mr. Shuang

  b 就了箇胖蘇娘
     (dzioù liau go) pàng sū niáng   tpp r
     Made off with a fat Miss Su;

2a   兩口兒便似熊模樣
     liāng koû (r̂) bièn sž hiúng mú iàng   xpxtppc r
     The two of them, just like great big bears,

  b 成就了風流喘豫章
     chiáng dzioù (liau) fūng lioú chiuên iù zhiāng   xtppttp r
     Their mad affair done, puffed for a while at
        Yü-chang;

2c   繡幃中一對兒鴛鴦象
     sioù uəî (zhūng) î. duəî (r̂) iuēn iāng siàng   xpxtppc r
     In bed they were a pair of elephantine love birds;

3   交肚皮廝撞[26]
     (gaū) dù pî sž zhuàng   xpxc r
     And when they coupled their bellies went ka-pung!

By rhyming p̀ang "fat" with Shuang lang and Su niang in his first reference to the ideal lovers, Wang Ting makes it clear that the allusion is hardly to be taken seriously. The humor of the assonance combined with the allusion in this first sentence would have to be translated into English something as follows: "A mountainous Montague

---

25. Jen Na, *Ch'ü-hsieh*, ii, pp. 64—68.
26. YJHLC has 教. I follow TPYF, ii, p. 11b, and CYSC.

eloped with a corpulent Capulet . . . ." After the first line the allusion
needs only token support. The imagination that inspired the last line
is typical of Wang Ting.

It is easy to underestimate the literary value of the geographical
allusion. Take, for example, the first four lines of the anonymous
Tao-tao ling discussed in Chapter 4 (pp. 94—95). There is a natural
sequence based on the four points of the compass: if we take Ch'ang-
an as the west, then Mang-shan, which is outside of Lo-yang, suggests the east, the Wu River is in the south, and Han-tan is in the
north. Allusion to such widely separated places gives the impression
that the poet is taking all of China into his view and summing up all
the events of history, and his statements about man, heroes, and fate
are made to sound universally true.

For example, the terms in these two lines by Ch'iao Chi (YJHLC,
p. 322; CYSC, p. 606),

載酒吴船
tsaĭ dzioŭ ú chiuān
Carry wine in a boat from Wu,

擊筑秦歌
gĭ. zhiŭ. tsián gō
Play the harp and sing songs from Ch'in.

all references to historical personages aside, bring elegance to the
lines. We must remember that as technical geographical designations
these terms originated before the Han dynasty, and that they were
used thereafter mainly as historical terms. The lines above should be
taken in the same light as, for instance, a Western poet's claim to be
singing "Northumbrian aires in an Aegean bark."

Apart from lending elegance or literary flavor to a poem, the geographical allusion can be as effective as vowel and consonant color
in suggesting ideas to the reader. The three historical terms in Chang
Yang-hao's poem function in this way. At the time he wrote, probably
1329, the last year of his life, he was an official in the district of
Kuan-chung, which was in the grip of famine.[27]

Chang Yang-hao (1269—1329): Chung lü, Shan p'o yang, "T'ung-kuan,
T'ung Pass." (YJHLC, p. 138; CYSC, p. 437)

1a   峯巒如聚
        fūng luón riŭ dziù   ppxc r
        Peaks as if massed,

---

27. Kuan-chung covers most of modern Shensi province, and T'ung-
kuan is on its eastern edge. See Chang Yang-hao's biography, *Yüan
shih*, clxxv, pp. 811—12.

b 波濤如怒
  buō taú riú nù   ppxc r
  Waves as if angry,

c 山河表裏潼關路
  shān hó biaû lî túng guān lù   xpxtppc r
  Along the mountains and the river lies the road
     to T'ung Pass.

2a 望西都
  vàng sī dū   tpp *r*
  I look to the West Capital,

b 意踟蹰[28]
  ì chî chiú   tpp r
  My thoughts unsettled;

3a 傷心秦漢經行處
  shiāng siām tsián hòn giāng hiáng chiù   xpxtppc r
  Here, where the Ch'in and Han armies passed,
     I lament

b 宮闕萬間都做了土
  gūng kiuê. vàn gān dū dzù (liau) tû   xtxppts r
  The ten thousand palaces, all turned to dust;

4a 興
  hiāng   p
  Kingdoms rise,

b 百姓苦
  baî. siàng kû   xcs r
  The people suffer;

5a 亡
  váng   p
  Kingdoms fall,

b 百姓苦
  baî. siàng kû   xcs r
  The people suffer.

T'ung Pass, because of its position between the cities of Ch'ang-an and Lo-yang, was a point of strategic importance, especially to those courts that had to keep out an encroaching enemy from the west. The West Capital is an archaic term full of the images of splendor but here there are connotations of decay as well. T'ung Pass on its own could be a neutral allusion, but by linking it with the Ch'in and Han

---

28. Here I follow TPYF. See CYSC, 438 n.

armies, Chang Yang-hao recalls the political instability and turmoil
that is a part of the rise and fall of kingdoms and establishes a frame-
work of circumstances in which the refrain "The people suffer" takes
on a special irony.

The treatment of detail takes no particular form but there is one
unusual technique that deserves comment. Quite often a writer will
present in his description a simple facade, almost as though he were
describing a picture. For example, in the line by Chang K'o-chiu
(full text on p. 107),

倚樹哀猿弄雲尖
ī shiù oī iuēn lùng iuə́n dziēm
In the trees, monkeys play with the
    tops of clouds . . .

it is difficult to explain how the poet could suggest that monkeys can
play with clouds. The only answer is that from the poet's vantage
point the monkeys in the trees are in line with the clouds in the background and their activity on the branches suggests playing with clouds.
The poet is describing the scene in two dimensions.[29]

Some of the most successful imagery is made through the imaginative choice and arrangement of detail. We have already seen several
examples of this but it is worthwhile to examine another poem to see
specifically in what manner details are arranged to achieve poetic
effect. For this we take as our example the most famous of all hsiao-
ling. It was attributed by a Ming dynasty critic to Ma Chih-yüan,
and of all Yüan writers he is undoubtedly most worthy of it, but Yüan
sources give no author:[30]

Anonymous: Yüeh tiao, T'ien ching sha, no title, but usually called
"Ch'iu ssu, Autumn Thoughts." (YJHLC, p. 391; CYSC, p. 242)

1a   枯藤老樹昏鴉
     kū táng laû shiù huə̄n á   xpxtpp   r
     Withered vines, an old tree, dusk, crows;

 b   小橋流水人家
     siaû kiaú lioú shuəî riə́n gā   xpxtpp   r
     A small bridge, flowing water, a few
         houses;

_____

    29. For a discussion of this in T'ang poetry, see Lin Yü-t'ang's
article "The Technique and Spirit of Chinese Poetry."

    30. See Chiang Yi-k'uei, *Yao shan t'ang ch'ü chi, Hsin ch'ü yüan*
edition, 2,ix:5a. It is also included with Ma Chih-yüan's songs in
both YJHLC and CYSC.

c   古道西風瘦馬
   gû daù sī fūng shoù mâ   xtpptx   r
   Ancient road, the west wind, a lean horse;

2a   夕陽西下
   sí. iáng sī hà   xpxt *r*
   Late sun sets in the west,

b   斷腸人在天涯
   duòn chiáng rián dzaì tiēn iá   xpxtpp r
   A heartbroken man at the ends of the earth.

Before discussing the treatment of detail it is important to consider the manner in which the natural climax of the verse form is emphasized. The short line interrupts the uniform flow of the first three lines, leading one to anticipate the last line in which the balance is restored. The short line of this particular verse shows contrasting vowel sounds as well, the *si* syllable, used twice, being a higher vowel than those dominating the first sentence. This contrast accentuates the imbalance in the verse so that when the last line returns to lower vowels and the length of the earlier lines, there is a greater sense of fitness in the conclusion of the poem.

The details of the poem appear gradually, like the features of a painted landscape as one opens a scroll.[31] This impression arises freely out of the syntax because no heavy subject-predicate or verb-object relationships encumber it. That verbs, usually essential to figurative language, have no active part, except in *sī hà* of line 2a, is the most striking feature of the style in this poem. The impersonal details in the first sentence are aspects of the scene the reader feels he can experience directly. Without verbs there is no question of the poet's interpreting the scene, as there can be, for example, in the second of the following two lines from a poem on the same theme in a different verse form, Tsui chung t'ien, but with the same diction and rhymes:[32]

      老樹懸藤掛
      laû shiù hién tźng guà
      On the old tree suspended vines hang,
      落日映殘霞
      luò. rì. iàng tsán há
      The setting sun reflects on wisps of cloud ...

---

31. This observation has been made by James Liu in *The Art of Chinese Poetry*, p. 42.

32. Anonymous: Hsien lü, Tsui chung t'ien, no title. (YJHLC, p. 36; CYSC, p. 1673).

Though the lines are evocative, the poet does not achieve the detachment of the first poem. The choice of adjectives like "withered, old, lean," in the first part of the T'ien ching sha, furthermore, suggest fatigue and travel-weariness which prepare the reader's mood for the last line. As a contrast, look at the two final lines of the Tsui chung t'ien:

夕陽西下
sí. iáng sī hà
Late sun sets in the west,

竹籬茅舍人家
(zhiû. lî) maú shiè rión gā
Bamboo fences, thatched huts,
　　—man's dwellings.

The ending trails off in details of description whereas the last line of the T'ien ching sha fixes the poem upon the nostalgia of the speaker, and although it is not a particularly striking line on its own, with its balance of sound and rhythm and its focus on a universal emotion it becomes the perfect conclusion to the poem.

Although the figures of speech discussed in this chapter present a cross-section of types, they do not necessarily represent the tendencies and preferences of san-ch'ü writers in their use of poetic devices; we may, however, make a few tentative conclusions about figures of speech in san-ch'ü. It is true that many are based on conventional associations, and it would appear that the san-ch'ü writer had no special concern for revelational figures of speech. This is particularly evident in noun substitutions even though many of them are enlivened through allegory. Expressed comparisons have their natural limitations but Chinese syntax offers advantages we cannot enjoy in Western languages, as Chang K'o-chiu's simple juxtaposition of elements showed in his "mountains" and "swords" figure. In the West we tend to emphasize the figure of speech with its syllogistic relationships; allusion receives somewhat more attention from the Chinese. On the other hand, the proper arrangement of detail, as we have just seen, can produce imagery equal to that of any of the other devices.

Reference Matter

List of Authors

(A nom de plume is given if in common use.)

Ah-li Hsi-ying 阿里西瑛, fl. 1300

Chang K'o-chiu 張可久 (Hsiao-shan 小山), ca. 1280–ca. 1330

Chang Yang-hao 張養浩 (Yun-chuang 雲莊), 1269–1329

Chao Ming-tao 趙明道, fl. 1279

Chao Shan-ch'ing 趙善慶, fl. 1320

Ch'iao Chi 喬吉 (Meng-fu 夢符), 1280–1345

Chou Te-ch'ing 周德清, fl. 1324

Chou Wen-chih 周文質, d. 1334

Hsieh Ang-fu 薛昂夫, fl. 1302

Hsü Tsai-ssu 徐再思 (T'ien-chai 甜齋), fl. 1300

Hu Chih-yü 胡祗遹 (1227–1293)

Jen Yü 任昱 (Tse-ming 則明), fl. 1331

Kuan Han-ch'ing 關漢卿, ca. 1220–ca. 1300

Kuan Yün-shih 貫雲石 (Suan-chai 酸齋), 1286–1324

Li Chih-yüan 李致遠, fl. 1354

Liu T'ing-hsin 劉庭信, fl. 1368

Lu Chih 盧摯 (Su-chai 疏齋), 1234–1300

Lü Chi-min 呂濟民, fl. 1302

Ma Chih-yüan 馬致遠 (Tung-li 東籬), ca. 1260–ca. 1324

129

Pai P'u 白樸 (Jen-fu 仁甫), b. 1226—d.?

Shang Cheng-shu 商政叔, fl. 1212

Sung Fang-hu 宋方壺, fl. 1317

Teng Yü-pin 鄧玉賓, fl. 1294

Tseng Jui 曾瑞 (Jui-ch'ing 瑞卿), fl. 1294

Tu Tsun-li 杜撙禮, fl. 1320

Wang Po-ch'eng 王伯成, fl. 1279

Wang Shih-fu 王實甫, fl. 1300

Wang Ting 王鼎 (Ho-ch'ing 和卿), fl. 1246

Ch'ü p'ai and Modes

An alphabetical list of verse forms mentioned in the text with most common alternate names:

Chai-er ling 寨兒令

Che kuei ling 折桂令 (Ch'an kung ch'u 蟾宮曲)

Ch'en tsui tung feng 沈醉東風

Ch'ing chiang yin 清江引

Ch'üeh t'a chih 鵲踏枝

Chu ma t'ing 駐馬聽

Ch'u t'ien yao 楚天遙

Hsiao liang chou 小梁州

Hsiao t'ao hung 小桃紅

Hsi ch'un lai 喜春來 (Yang ch'un ch'ü 陽春曲)

Hsin shui ling 新水令

Huang chung wei 黃鍾尾

Hung hsiu hsieh 紅繡鞋 (Chu lü ch'ü 朱履曲)

Luo mei feng 落梅風 (Shou yang ch'ü 壽陽曲)

Ma lang-er yao p'ien 麻郎兒么篇

Pai ho-tzu 白鶴子

P'o pu tuan 撥不斷

P'u t'ien lo 普天樂

131

Sai hung ch'iu 塞鴻秋
Shang hua shih 賞花時
Shan p'o yang 山坡羊
Shui hsien-tzu 水仙子
Ssu k'uai yü 四塊玉
Tao-tao ling 叨叨令
Ta te ko 大德歌
Tien ch'ien huan 殿前歡
T'ien ching sha 天淨沙
Tou an ch'un 鬭鵪鶉
Tsui chung t'ien 醉中天
Tsui t'ai-p'ing 醉太平
Wu yeh-er 梧葉兒
Yi chih hua 一枝花
Ying hsien k'o 迎仙客
Yüeh chin ching 閱金經

The nine modes in most common use are given first:

Cheng kung 正宮
Chung lü 中呂
Hsien lü 仙呂
Huang chung 黃鍾
Nan lü 南呂
Shang tiao 商調
Shuang tiao 雙調
Ta-shih tiao 大石調
Yüeh tiao 越調

Hsiao-shih tiao 小石調
Shang chiao tiao 商角調
Pan she tiao 般涉調

Bibliography

Abbreviations of frequently cited works

CKKT   *Chung-kuo ku-tien hsi-ch'ü lun chu chi ch'eng*
CKSCS   *Chung-kuo san-ch'ü shih.* See Luo Chin-t'ang
CYSC   *Ch'üan yüan san-ch'ü*
CYYY   *Chung-yüan yin-yün.* See Chou Te-ch'ing
HYSLH   *Han-yü shih-lü hsüeh.* See Wang Li
SCTK   *San-ch'ü ts'ung k'an*
SPTK   *Ssu pu ts'ung k'an*
TPYF   *Ch'ao-yeh hsin sheng t'ai-p'ing yüeh-fu*
TTSFSC   *Tso tz'u shih fa shu cheng*
YCPH   *Yang ch'un pai hsüeh*
YFCC   *Yüeh-fu ch'ün chu*
YFCY   *Yüeh-fu ch'ün yü*
YFHS   *Yüeh-fu hsin sheng*
YJHLC   *Yüan jen hsiao-ling chi*

The Book of Odes. Translated by Bernard Karlgren. Stockholm, 1950.

Brooke-Rose, Christine. *A Grammar of Metaphor.* London, 1958.

Chang Hsiang 張相. *Shih tz'u ch'ü yü-tz'u hui-shih* 詩詞曲語辭匯釋. Reprint. Taipei, 1962.

Chao Ching-shen 趙景深. "Chou te-ch'ing te hsiao-ling ting ko 周德清的小令定格." This is an article in his *Tu ch'ü hsiao chi* 讀曲小集. Shanghai, 1959.

Ch'ao-yeh hsin sheng t'ai-p'ing yüeh-fu 朝野新聲太平樂府 (TPYF). Edited by Yang Chao-ying 楊朝英 (fl. 1300). Facsimile of Yüan edition. In SPTK. There is also an edition annotated by Lu Chi-yeh. Peking, 1955.

Cheng Chen-to 鄭振鐸. *Ch'a t'u pen chung-kuo wen-hsüeh shih* 插圖本中國文學史. 2 vols. Peking, 1959.

———. *Chung-kuo su wen-hsüeh shih* 中國俗文學史. Peking, 1959.

Cheng Ch'ien 鄭騫. *Ts'ung shih tao ch'u* 從詩到曲. Taipei, 1961.

Ch'en Wang-tao 陳望道. *Hsiu-tz'u hsüeh fa fan* 修辭學發凡. Shanghai, 1954.

Chiang Yi-k'uei 蔣一葵 (15th–16th c.). *Yao shan t'ang ch'ü chi* 堯山堂曲紀. Reprint. In *Hsin ch'ü yüan.*

Chou Fa-kao 周法高. "Shuo p'ing-tse 說平仄." *Chung-yang yen-chiu yüan, li-shih yü-yen yen-chiu suo chi k'an* 中央研究院歷史語言研究所集刊 13 (1948):153–62.

Chou Te-ch'ing 周德清 (fl. 1324). *Chung-yüan yin-yün* 中原音韻 (CYYY). 2 chüan. The edition used is the reprint of 1926, n.p., with Ch'en Nai-ch'ien's calligraphy on the title page. There are several editions and reprints. For a description of them, see Stimson, Hugh, "The Phonology of the *Chung-yüan yin-yün.*" Another annotated reprint is found in CKKT, 1:183–285.

Chou Ts'e-tsung 周策縱. "Ting hsing hsin-shih t'i te t'i-yi 定形新詩體的提議." *World Forum* 海外論壇 3, no. 9 (1962):2–14.

Ch'üan sung tz'u 全宋詞. Edited by T'ang Kuei-chang 唐圭璋. 5 vols. Peking, 1965.

Ch'üan t'ang shih 全唐詩. Compiled by Ts'ao Yen 曹寅 (ca. 1707). Reprint. 16 vols. Taipei, 1961.

Ch'üan yüan san-ch'ü 全元散曲 (CYSC). Edited by Sui Shu-shen 隨樹森. 2 vols. Peking, 1964.

Chu Ch'üan 朱權 (d. 1448). *T'ai-ho cheng yin p'u* 太和正音譜. Annotated reprint. In CKKT, 3:1–231.

Chu Chü-yi 朱居易. *Yüan chü su-yü fang-yen li shih* 元劇俗語方言例釋. Shanghai, 1956.

Ch'ü hsieh. See Jen Na.

Chung-kuo ku-tien hsi-ch'ü lun chu chi ch'eng 中國古典戲曲論著集成 (CKKT). Edited under the auspices of the Chung-kuo hsi-ch'ü yen-chiu yüan 中國戲曲研究院. 10 vols. Peking, 1959. A most useful collection of source material on ch'ü. Reprint. Hongkong, n.d.

Chung-kuo wen-hsüeh shih 中國文學史. Edited under the auspices of the Chung-kuo k'o-hsüeh yüan wen-hsüeh yen-chiu suo 中國科學院 文學研究所. 3 vols. Peking, 1962. Also referred to as K'o-hsüeh yüan *Chung-kuo wen-hsüeh shih*.

Ch'ü yüan 曲苑. n.p., 1921. Most of the articles in it are now reprinted in CKKT.

Ehr-shih-liu shih 二十六史. Taipei, 1961–65.

Fu Li-p'u 傅隸樸. *Chung-kuo yün-wen kai lun* 中國韻文概論. 2 vols. Taipei, 1954.

Goodman, Paul. *The Structure of Literature*. Chicago, 1962.

Hoffman, Alfred. "Kurze Einführung in die Technik der *San-ch'ü*." *Chung-te hsueh-pao* 中德學報 5 (1943):119–35.

Hsin chiao chiu chüan pen yang ch'un pai hsüeh (cited as *Hsin chiao chiu chüan pen* YCPH) 新校九卷本陽春白雪. Annotated by Sui Shu-shen. 9 chüan. Peking, 1957. Reprint (under the title *Chiu chüan pen yang ch'un pai hsüeh chiao chu* ... 校注). Taipei, 1960. The pagination is the same in both but the annotator's name is deleted along with some useful information regarding the discovery of this, the nine-chüan edition of the *Yang ch'un pai hsüeh*, by Sui Shu-shen before 1949 in Nanking.

Hsin ch'ü yüan 新曲苑. Edited by Jen Na. Shanghai, 1940.

Hsü Chia-jui 徐嘉瑞. *Chin yüan hsi-ch'ü fang-yen k'ao* 金元戲曲 方言考. Shanghai, 1956. First published before 1949. Reprint (author given as Hsü K'un-hua 昆華). Taipei, 1962.

Hsü K'un-hua. See Hsü Chia-jui.

Jen Ehr-pei 任二北 [Jen Na]. *Tun-huang ch'ü chiao lu* 敦煌曲校錄. Shanghai, 1955.

Jen Na 任訥. *Ch'ü hsieh* 曲諧. 4 chüan. In SCTK, vol. 4.

——. *San-ch'ü kai lun* 散曲概論. 2 chüan. In SCTK, vol. 4.

——. *Tz'u ch'ü t'ung yi* 詞曲通義. Reprint. Hongkong, 1964. The
author's name is deleted from this edition.

K'o-hsüeh yüan *Chung-kuo wen-hsüeh shih*. See *Chung-kuo wen-
hsüeh shih*.

Lao-tzu tao-te ching 老子道德經. In SPTK.

Levis, John Hazedel. *Foundations of Chinese Musical Art*. Peiping,
1936.

Liang Shu 梁書. See *Ehr-shih-liu shih*.

Liang T'ing-nan 梁廷枏 (1795–1861). *Ch'ü hua* 曲話. 5 chüan. Reprint in *Ch'ü yüan*. Also in CKKT, 8:238–95. Reprinted in separate
volume. Taipei, 1965.

Lin Yü-t'ang. "The Technique and Spirit of Chinese Poetry." *Journal
of the China Branch of the Royal Asiatic Society* 66(1935):33–34.

Liu, James T. Y. *The Art of Chinese Poetry*. Chicago, 1966.

Liu Ta-chieh 劉大杰. *Chung-kuo wen-hsüeh fa-chan shih* 中國文學
發展史. 3 vols. Hongkong, 1964.

Li Yü 李玉 (fl. 1644). *Yi li an pei tz'u kuang cheng p'u* 一笠庵北詞
廣正譜. Published by Ch'ing lien shu wu 青蓮書屋, n.p., n.d.

Li yüan an shih yüeh-fu hsin sheng 梨園按試樂府新聲 (YFHS). 3
chüan. Facsimile of Yüan edition. In SPTK *hsü pien*. There is
also an edition annotated by Sui Shu-shen. Peking, 1958.

Lu Chih-wei 陸志韋. *Shih yün p'u* 詩韻譜. *Yenching Journal of Chinese Studies* Monograph Series, no. 21. Peking, 1948. Reprint.
Hongkong, 1966.

Lu Chi-yeh 盧冀野. *Tz'u ch'ü yen-chiu* 詞曲研究. Hongkong, 1963.

Luo Chin-t'ang 羅錦堂. *Chung-kuo san-ch'ü shih* 中國散曲史 (CKSCS).
2 vols. Taipei, 1957.

——. *Pei ch'ü hsiao-ling p'u* 北曲小令譜. Hongkong, 1964.

Luo K'ang-lieh 羅慷烈. *Pei hsiao-ling wen-tzu p'u* 北小令文字譜.
    Hongkong, 1962.

Nan pei kung tz'u chi 南北宮詞紀. Edited by Ch'en Suo-wen 陳所聞
    (d. ca. 1604). *Nan kung tz'u chi*, 6 chüan; *Pei kung tz'u chi*, 6
    chüan. Modern edition annotated by Chao Ching-shen. 4 vols.
    Peking, 1959.

Pei tz'u kuang cheng p'u. See Li Yü.

P'ei wen yün fu 佩文韻府 (1711). 106 chüan. The edition used is
    the *Ch'in ting p'ei wen yün fu* 欽定 .... 200 ts'e. Shanghai, 1892.

San-ch'ü ts'ung k'an 散曲叢刊 (SCTK). Edited by Jen Na. 4 vols.
    Taipei, 1964.

Sheng shih hsin sheng 盛世新聲. 12 chüan. Photo-reprint of 1517
    edition. Peking, 1955.

Shih-chi. See Ssu-ma Ch'ien.

Shih chi chüan 詩集傳. Annotated by Chu Hsi 朱熹 (1130–1200). In
    SPTK.

Ssu-ma Ch'ien 司馬遷 (B.C. 145–86). *Shih chi* 史記. Annotated by
    Ku Chieh-kang 顧頡剛. 10 vols. Peking, 1959.

Ssu pu ts'ung k'an 四部叢刊 (SPTK). Shanghai, 1920–22. Also the
    hsü pien 續編. Shanghai, 1934–35.

Stimson, Hugh. *The Jongyuan In Yunn*. Sinological Series, no. 12.
    New Haven, 1966.

——. "The Phonology of the *Chung-yüan yin-yün*." *Tsing Hua Jour-
    nal of Chinese Studies*, n.s. 3, no. 1 (1962):114–59.

T'ang Yüeh 唐鉞. *Kuo ku hsin t'an* 國故新探. 3 chüan. Shanghai,
    1926. Reprint. Taipei, 1966.

T'ao Tsung-yi 陶宗儀 (fl. 1360). *Ch'o keng lu* 輟耕錄. 30 chüan.
    Reprint. Taipei, 1963.

T'ao yüan-ming chi 陶淵明集. Edited by Li Kung-huan 李公煥. In
    SPTK.

Ts'ai pi ch'ing tz'u 彩筆情辭. Edited by Chang Hsü 張栩 (fl. 1500).
    12 chüan. Also called *Ch'ing lou yün yü kuang chi* 青樓韻語廣集.
    Neither edition available to me.

Tso tz'u shih fa shu cheng 作詞十法疏證 (TTSFSC). Annotated by
    Jen Na. In SCTK, vol. 4. This is a most useful edition of Chou
    Te-ch'ing's "Tso tz'u shih fa" ("Ten Rules for Writing Tz'u"), the
    last section in CYYY, chüan ii.

Tz'u lin chai yen 詞林摘豔. Edited by Chang Lu 張祿. 10 chüan.
    Photo-reprint of 1525 edition. 2 vols. Peking, 1955.

Wang Ch'in-hsi 王琴希. "Sung tz'u shang-ch'ü-sheng tzu yü hsi-
    ch'ü kuan-hsi ji ssu-sheng-t'i k'ao-cheng 宋詞上去聲字與戲曲
    關係及四聲體芳證" *Wen shih* 文史 2 (1963):139–62.

Wang Ching-ch'ang 汪經昌. *Ch'ü hsüeh li shih* 曲學例釋. Taipei,
    1966.

Wang Chi-te 王驥德 (d. 1623). *Ch'ü lü* 曲律. 4 chüan. Reprint. In
    CKKT, 4:43–191.

Wang Li 王力. *Han-yü shih-lü hsüeh* 漢語詩律學 (HYSLH). 2d ed.
    Shanghai, 1962.

Wang Shih-chen 王世貞 (1526–1590). *Ch'ü tsao* 曲藻. Reprint. In
    CKKT, 4:27–42.

Wang Shih-fu 王實甫 (fl. 1300). *Hsi hsiang chi* 西廂記. Reprint.
    In *Yüan ch'ü hsüan wai pien*, 1:259–323.

Wen hsüan 文選. Edited by Hsiao T'ung 蕭統 (501–531). Facsimile
    of Sung edition. In SPTK.

Wu Hsiao-ling 吳曉鈴. *Kuan han-ch'ing hsi-ch'ü chi* 關漢卿戲曲集.
    Peking, 1958.

Wu Mei 吳梅. *Ku ch'ü chu t'an* 顧曲塵談. 2 chüan. Shanghai, 1926.

Wu Nan-hsün 吳南薰. *Lü-hsüeh huei t'ung* 律學會通. Peking, 1964.

Yang ch'un pai hsüeh 陽春白雪 (YCPH). Edited by Yang Chao-ying
    (ca. 1340). 10 chüan. Facsimile of Yüan edition. Basic Sinological

Series. Shanghai, 1936. There is also an edition annotated by Jen Na in SCTK, vol. 1.

Yin hung yi suo k'o ch'ü 飲虹簃所刻曲. Edited by Lu Chi-yeh. Originally printed by the editor, 1932. Reprint. 2 vols. Taipei, 1961.

Yoshikawa Kojiro 吉川幸次郎. *Yüan tsa-chu yen-chiu* 元雜劇研究. Translated by Cheng Ch'ing-mao 鄭清茂. Taipei, 1960.

Yüan ch'ü hsüan 元曲選. Edited by Tsang Mao-shun 藏懋循 (fl. 1580). Reprint. 4 vols. Peking, 1958.

Yüan ch'ü hsüan wai pien .... 外編. Edited by Sui Shu-shen. 3 vols. Peking, 1959.

Yüan jen hsiao-ling chi 元人小令集 (YJHLC). Edited by Ch'en Nai-ch'ien 陳乃乾. Peking, 1962.

Yüan shih 元史. See *Ehr-shih-liu shih*.

Yüeh-fu ch'ün chu 樂府羣珠 (YFCC). 4 chüan. Original edition dates from Ming. Editor unknown. Modern edition annotated by Lu Chi-yeh. Shanghai, 1955. Reprint. Taiwan, 1961.

Yüeh-fu ch'ün yü 樂府羣玉 (YFCY). Probably edited by Hu Ts'un-shan 胡存善 (ca. 1300). 5 chüan. Reprint. In SCTK, vol. 1.

Yüeh-fu hsin sheng. See *Li yüan an shih yüeh-fu hsin sheng*.

Yung-hsi yüeh-fu 雍熙樂府. Probably edited by Kuo Hsun 郭勛 (ca. 1500). 20 chüan. Facsimile of edition printed between 1522 and 1566. In SPTK *hsü pien*.

Index

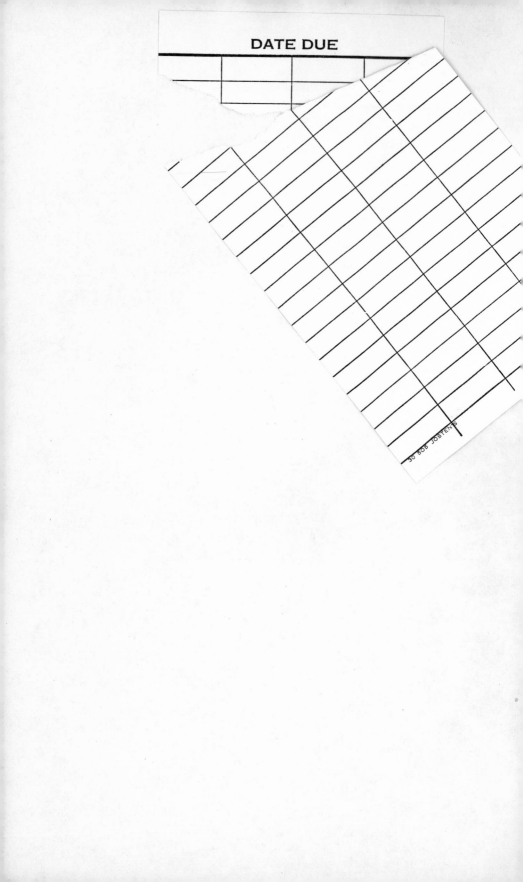

DATE DUE

30 505 JOSTENS